All About Our New Cookbook

Following the success of Squirrels Cookbooks One and Two and the many requests we have received for both books, we decided it would be a good idea to incorporate the best of both into one book... and here it is!

All the recipes are tried and true, having been served at one time or another at Squirrels restaurant and reflect a variety of tastes, textures and flavours. For those starting out on the path of vegetarian cuisine the recipes are easy to follow while a description of exotic or lesser-known ingredients is given in the book, as well as where to get them.

For those seeking new taste sensations or simply good solid menus to add to their repertoire, there is an abundance of material from soups to desserts.

We have also included some practical nutritional information for those concerned about healthy eating.

BON APPÉTIT!

PUBLISHER

Diana Mitchell
Squirrells Australia Pty. Ltd.
A.C.N. 010 122 237
PO Box 287
West End
QLD 4101
PH: 368 3400 A/H 368 1838
MOBILE: 018 738 738

PRINTER

The Book Printer
Suite 105
83 Longueville Road
Lane Cove
NSW
PH: (02) 427 3533

ISBN 0 646 01913 9

Squirrels Cookbooks Nos One and Two were written and illustrated by Vicki Jackson, who worked at Squirrels for five years before she got distracted by Sydney, books and bakery speculations.

Antoinette Waters, a professional artist and illustrator who lives in a Brisbane bayside suburb with three Russian Wolfhounds, wrote the additional text and created the new illustrations and cover art for
    Squirrels Best of One and Two
    Vegetarian Cookbooks

NUTRITION in a NUTSHELL

By Amanda Benham Vegan and Vegetarian from the Societies of Australia

How do you survive on a vegetarian diet?

Many people feel concerned that giving up meat will create nutritional problems. It's a strange thing that when people eat meat, fish and poultry, they don't worry whether these foods have sufficient nutrition in them. It's only when they change to a vegetarian diet that they suddenly realize that food is for nutrition.

The typical reaction a vegetarian encounters in polite conversation is, how do you find anything to eat? and where do you get your protein?

Vegetarianism is not just the giving up of meat eating - it's an introduction to a whole new range of foods which you have never previously tasted nor cooked and which can be made into a delicious range of meals.

Science has proven that a properly chosen vegetarian diet has all the nutrients we need, whatever our age.

What are the Advantages and Benefits of a Vegetarian Diet?

A Vegetarian diet offers a diet which is
- low in cholesterol (a vegan diet is cholesterol-free)
- low in saturated fat
- high in fibre
- loaded with vitamins and minerals

Vegetarians in general are slimmer than meat-eaters and suffer less from many diseases including heart disease, stroke, high blood pressure, diabetes, osteoporosis, kidney stones, diverticular disease, gallstones and some cancers.

Some 60% of Australians die of diet-related causes which are in many cases preventable. A good vegetarian diet offers protection from "diseases of affluence" so in general vegetarians live longer, healthier lives than meat-eaters.

Avoiding the overuse of salt, sugar, fat and alcohol will make your vegetarian diet even better!

A Vegetarian diet makes better use of the world's resources, doing less damage to the environment and enabling more people to be fed than a diet containing meat. Plus vegetarians don't have to feel guilty when they pass an abattoir, and they never have to buy steak knives.

Where do vegetarians get their nutrients from?

There are some nutrients which people tend to associate with meat, eggs or dairy products, so that they mistakenly think that a diet without these must be lacking. But this isn't true! Protein, iron, calcium and vitamin B_{12} are the nutrients which people sometimes think have to come from animal products. However, modern nutritional wisdom has revealed otherwise.

Protein

Protein is important for growth and makes up about 20% of the body's structure. Proteins have other functions including acting as enzymes, hormones and antibodies. Our bodies' protein is continually being 'turned over' or renewed. Everyone needs protein, but most people on a typical 'western' diet get far more than they need.

Protein is widespread in foods; even tomatoes and oranges contain protein. It used to be thought that plant sources of protein had to be carefully combined to be effective. However it's now been found that provided a diet is varied and not excessively high in fat or sugar it will contain enough protein if it contains sufficient energy. (Calories/kilojoules.) Humans can get all their protein needs from plants, just like elephants, horses, kangaroos and lots of other animals do.

Some advocates of meat-eating argue that plant protein is 'inferior' or not as 'complete' as animal protein. But different types of plant protein complement each other, providing our body with ample good quality protein for it's needs. A high-protein plant-based diet can be obtained by choosing foods each day from each of the lists below.

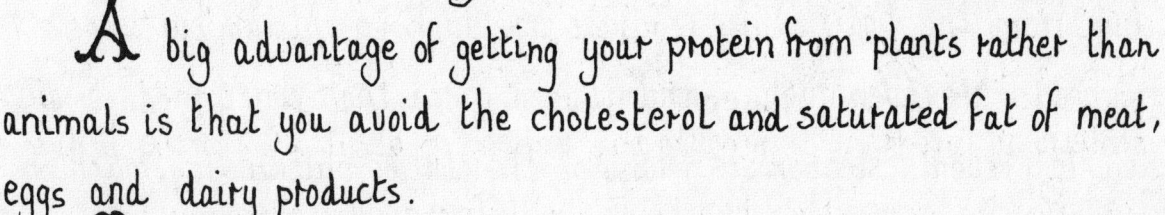

① Legumes
(e.g. beans, peas, lentils, tofu, tempeh)
Nuts
Seeds

② Grains
(e.g. bread, rice, pasta, flour wheat, rye, barley oats, corn etc.)

A big advantage of getting your protein from plants rather than animals is that you avoid the cholesterol and saturated fat of meat, eggs and dairy products.

Iron

Iron is needed by the body to enable haemoglobin in the blood to carry oxygen into tissues. Women of childbearing age have the highest requirement for iron, as they lose iron each month in their menstrual loss. Pregnant and breastfeeding women also need extra iron.

Fortunately it is not difficult to get enough iron from a vegetarian diet. Vegetarian foods rich in iron include:

wheat bran,	yeast	nuts
parsley	soy beans	dried figs
spinach	sesame seeds	apricots and peaches

Vitamin C enhances iron absorption, making more of the iron in food able to be used by the body. So having a glass of orange juice with your breakfast cereal or squeezing lemon juice onto spinach makes good nutritional sense.

Calcium

Calcium is needed for bone formation and has other functions, including being involved in blood coagulation, nerve transmission and muscle contraction. Pregnant and breastfeeding women need a higher than usual calcium intake to supply their growing babies.

A diet high in protein, especially animal protein, increases the loss of calcium from the body. Dairy products are high in calcium but some plant foods are even higher, and it is a myth that dairy products are needed to prevent osteoporosis. Many of the world's cultures (e.g. much of Asia) have traditionally never used dairy products, and may have quite low calcium diets, yet it is westerners that are the most afflicted by osteoporosis.

Plant foods rich in calcium include:

- sesame seeds (+ tahini)
- tofu
- soybeans
- almonds
- parsley
- treacle
- green vegetables
- fortified soymilk (e.g. So Good)

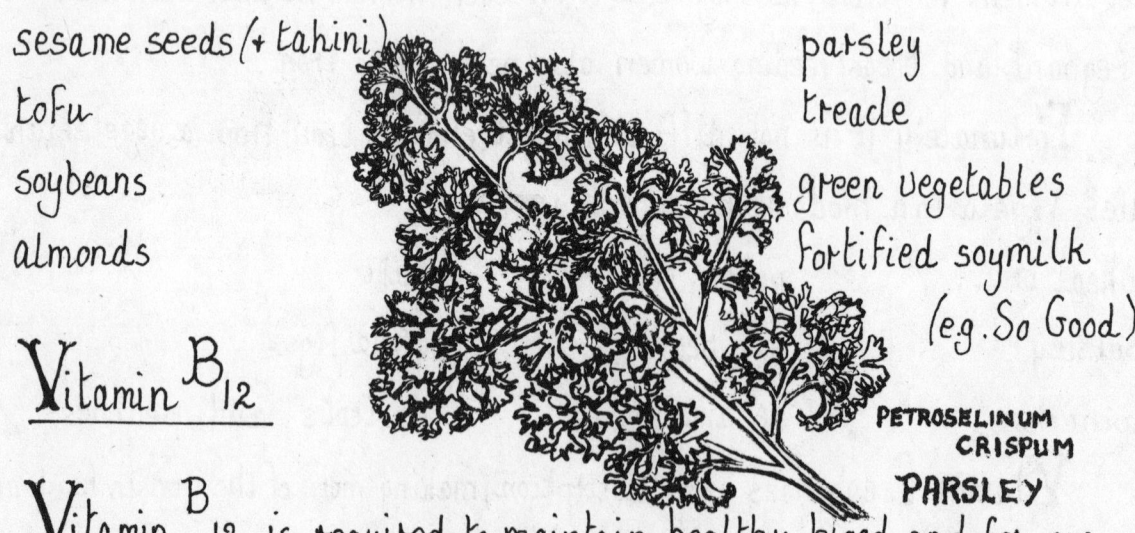

PETROSELINUM CRISPUM
PARSLEY

Vitamin B$_{12}$

Vitamin B$_{12}$ is required to maintain healthy blood and for our nervous system, and for detoxifying cyanide from food and cigarette smoke. Our bodies produce vitamin B$_{12}$ in the small intestine, but it appears that most of us are unable to make use of this source, and so need to get vitamin B12 from our diets. The amount required is actually very small, and our livers can store enough for around 2 to 10 years.

Most animal products contain vitamin B12, but it is also found in some plant foods. Fermented foods such as tempeh and miso contain vitamin B12, and it has been found in seaweeds and in the soil micro-organisms associated with unwashed vegetables. However, the amount found in these sources varies, so for vegans a reliable daily source such as a supplement or fortified soymilk (e.g. So Good) is a wise precaution.

Other nutrients in a Vegetarians diet

The other B-group vitamins are quite widespread in foods, and good non-animal sources include wheat bran, cornflakes, sesame seeds, yeast, nuts, soybeans and vegetables.

Vitamin A is obtained in the form of B-carotene from fruit and vegetables, especially carrots, pumpkin, green vegetables, apricots, mangoes, pawpaws and rockmelons

Vitamin C is also obtained from fruit and vegetables. It is high in currants, citrus fruits, strawberries, pineapple, capsicum, tomatoes and leafy green vegetables.

Vitamin D is high in table margarine, butter, eggs and cheese. However, in sunny Australia a dietary source of vitamin D is generally unneccessary, as our bodies make vitamin D in the skin when exposed to ultraviolet light or sunlight.

<u>Vitamin E</u> is widespread in foods and is especially high in oils, nuts and avocadoes.

<u>Vitamin K</u> is made by our own bodies, and is also high in vegetables.

<u>Zinc and other minerals</u> are obtained in a vegetarian diet from nuts, grains, yeast and vegetables.

How Do You Plan a Vegetarian Diet?

To ensure a well-balanced vegetarian diet, whether or not eggs and/or dairy products are included, choose foods each day from the following groups:

<u>LEGUMES, NUTS, SEEDS</u> (2+ SERVINGS)
- beans (e.g. haricot, kidney, Lima, borlotti, soy beans etc.)
- lentils
- peas (e.g. chickpeas)
- nuts
- tofu
- tempeh
- seeds (e.g. sesame, sunflower, pepitas)
- soymilk

<u>VEGETABLES</u> (4+ SERVINGS)
- green leafy vegetables
- yellow vegetables
- other vegetables
- sprouted seeds

<u>GRAINS, CEREALS</u> (2+ SERVINGS)
- rice
- pasta
- bread
- savoury biscuits
- oats
- millet
- barley
- rye
- wheat
- other grains

<u>FRUIT</u> (2+ SERVINGS)
- fresh fruit
- fruit juice
- dried fruit
- stewed fruit

<u>FATS</u> (1+ SERVINGS)
- PREF. vegetable oils (choose polyunsaturated or monounsaturated)
- vegetable margarine (polyunsaturated)

PREFACE

Awareness of vegetarian and vegan cuisine is at an all time high. In the last few years the world has been going through a quiet revolution in eating habits owing to increased concern about health, animal rights, and the environment. So how has this come about?

For a start human beings were never the huge meat eaters that popular mythology has made them. Throughout history humans have survived most successfully on agriculture as opposed to hunting; gathering and growing enough plant protein for the survival of their tribe or village and allowing them to store food for times of hardship. When the industrial revolution occurred advances in machinery allowed for such great yields of crops that there were enormous surpluses. Rather than wasting these crops they were fed to animals, creating an expanding market for animal produce.

Perhaps it is our awareness of the environment which is the fastest growing reason for the renewed interest in vegetarianism. The news that vast forests in Central America are being burnt or felled to graze cattle for the North American hamburger market, that a major contribution to acid rain in Europe is the growth of intensive farming of pigs and cattle, that the effluent from intensive animal agriculture and abbattoirs is a large factor in the pollution of our environment, have become of concern to all of us. Vegetarianism is the most ecologically sound diet available.

It takes over 10 times more land to produce a typical meat oriented diet than to produce a vegetarian one. Animals raised for food must be fed far more protein than they actually produce. It requires from 5 to

20 kilos of plant protein to produce one kilo of animal protein. About half of the world's grain crop is fed to animals which are raised for food, representing an enormous waste of food in a world where about two thirds of the population are hungry.

And of course there are the animals themselves. They are the largely forgotten link in the chain of food production. The '80's have seen a vast shift in public attitudes towards the welfare of animals. More people are buying free-range eggs and non animal tested cosmetics in an attempt to stop the cruelty involved, while others are taking one more step by not eating animals.

Whatever the reason, the vegetarian way of life is an important contributor in the development of a healthy, humane and equitable world.

Mark Berriman
President, The Australian Vegetarian Society.

RAISIN APPLE CAKE

Method: Cream together 2 oz (50 g) margarine and 5 oz (125 g) of castor sugar. Sift in 3 oz (75 g) of raising flour. Add a pinch of salt. Add 6 tbsp (6 × 15 ml sp) of milk gradually. Mix well and stir in 3 oz (150 g) self-raising flour. Add a pinch of salt. Add 6 tbsp (6 × 15 ml sp) of milk gradually. Mix well and Peel and slice 1 lb (400 g) of raisins. Spoon the mixture into a greased square 7½" (18.5 cm) shallow tin. with 1 oz (25 g) of castor sugar and 1 teaspoon (1 × 5 ml sp) of cinnamon. Bake in a pre-heated oven 190°C/375°F, Gas Mark 5 for 35 minutes. Turn onto a wire rack to cool.

TO COOK IN A MICROWAVE OVEN
The timings given are for a 650W machine.
Method: Prepare as in method above, spoon the mixture into a 7½" (18.5 cm) square shallow non-metallic tray. Peel and slice 1 lb (400 g) of Bramley apples. Arrange on top of the cake mixture. Sprinkle with 1 oz (25 g) of castor sugar and 1 tsp (1 × 5 ml sp) of cinnamon. Cook on full power for 8 minutes. Stand in tray for 2 minutes before turning out.

...the closure of 'Squirrels' at South Brisbane ...nning of 1994, Brisbane was desperate ...vegetarian restaurant. 'Garbanzos Garden' ...n restaurant, opened at Newmarket in ...of 1993. This restaurant has recently changed ...d Amanda and Alison bring you the new ...of Newmarket.

...endeavour to provide our customers with an environmentally positive outlook, and a nutritious, healthy and, of course, delicious menu. We don't use any animal products in our food, and offer a range of international dishes to please the most discerning palate.

Do the environment and your taste buds a favour and treat yourself at the new 'Squirrels of Newmarket.'
See you soon,
184 Enoggera Rd, Newmarket 856 0766   Alison + Amanda

Cooking with stainless steel

During the last couple of years, I have been using a product that I believe should have a special mention in my book, and that's the Dine-Rite cooking system.

Over the years, I have used many different types of cookware, both commercially in my restaurants and also at home, and none of them have proved to be as effective as the Dine-Rite cooking system. Let me tell you why:—

Firstly, you must understand that food presentation and cooking is a big job. For example, the average homemaker will spend 500 000 hours in the kitchen! Now, if a job is that big, and going to take up that much time, I think it only makes sense that we take the time and find the right equipment. Could you imagine going to a mechanic that doesn't have all the appropriate equipment to do the job? These days, NO!!!

Well, I think the same thing applies to our kitchens. Why not have the best equipment possible up front? The Dine-Rite system will save time spent in the kitchen, save on valuable nutrients, save on the energy used, and is the one system that does not need to be replaced constantly.

Now that you're thinking along the lines of what the right equipment is, let me tell you why I think Dine-Rite is so good:—

* The construction of the utensils: The Dine-Rite cooking system is constructed of a variety of metals sandwiched together.

* on the outside, and the inside that is in contact with heat and food, is a high quality stainless steel. On the inside, is a combination of alloys. The reasoning behind this is that stainless steel is an excellent metal to use for the presentation, durability point, but it does not conduct heat well. However by sandwiching the alloys inbetween the stainless steel, they have created a metal that lasts forever, is sanitary and conducts the heat not only across the bottom, but up the sides as well.

Because of this unique construction, Dine-Rite can offer a "LIFETIME GUARANTEE" on all their cooking utensils.

* the versatility of the utensils: I have introduced the cookware as the "Dine-Rite Cooking System". Well, that's exactly what it is. It's not just saucepans. For instance, the basic set will make up into 6 saucepans, 2 frypans, 4 dutch ovens, 5 casserole dishes, 2 steamer sets, 2 poaching sets, 2 double boilers, 6 serving pieces, 4 cake tins and many more combinations than I can remember. All this stacks into 20" of cupboard space.

See what I mean by a cooking system and not just saucepans. You can bake a cake in the system, you can fry fatless, you can even do a casserole on top of the stove and then serve the piece straight to the table.

* the waterless method: it's been proven that no other method of cooking retains more vitamins and nutrients than this method.

To find out more about Dine-Rite, contact Tracey Cunningham on 891 5699 or call personally at 6 Vanda St, Buranda, Queensland.

DIPS AND SPREADS

Many health food stores, delicatessens and supermarkets supply vegetarian patés and dips. Hommus and babaganouse for example are readily available.

FALAFEL MIX
A herbed chickpea croquette delight is also available already made up for convienience.

PURE HARVEST
ramen instant noodles for ease and convenience without the MSG.

VEGAN MARGARINE
A variety of margarines are now available without animal products, cholesterole and salt.

- woolworths home brand.
- becel
- nutalex

TOFU AND TEMPEH
is easy to prepare and can be added to simple vegetable dishes to give it an extra lift.

Vegetarian and Vegan Societies

Queensland

The Australian Vegetarian Society (QLD)
PO Box 400, South Brisbane, QLD 4101 PH 07 893-2323

The Vegan Society of Brisbane
PO Box 400, South Brisbane, QLD 4101 PH (07) 893-2323

Tableland Vegetarian Society
PO Box 25, Millaa Millaa QLD 4886

The Vegan Society (Sunshine Coast)
PO Box 255, Noosa Heads, QLD 4567 PH (074) 490521

Western Australia

The Vegetarian Society of Western Australia
PO Box 220, North Perth, WA 6006. PH (09) 275-5682

South Australia

The Vegetarian Society of South Australia
PO Box 46, Rundle Mall, Adelaide, 5000
PH (08) 261-3194

Vegetarian and Vegan Societies

NEW SOUTH WALES

The Australian Vegetarian Society (NSW)
PO Box 65, Paddington, NSW 2021, PH (02) 698 4339

The Vegan Society (NSW)
PO Box 467, Broadway, NSW 2007 PH (02) 436-1373

The Jewish Vegetarian Society (NSW)
C/- Tom Kramer 95/97 The Boulevarde, Strathfield, NSW 2135
PH (02) 642-3110 (AH) or (02) 683 5991 (BH)

The Australian Natural Hygiene Society, "Hygia"
31 Cobar Road, Arcadia, NSW 2159
PH (02) 653-1115 or (02) 651-2457

VICTORIA

The Australian Vegetarian Society (VIC)
PO Box 226, North Melbourne, VIC 3051
PH (03) 329 1374

Vegan Society of Australia
PO Box 85, Seaford, Vic 3198   PH (03) 786 6192

The Vegetarian Information Centre
PO Box 440, Richmond Vic 3121

A GUIDE THRU THE DIET MAZE

Vegetarian – a general term for people who don't eat any meat or fish – often mistaken for people who don't eat red meat but do eat fish & chicken, but they're not really vegetarians.

Ovo-Lacto Vegetarians will eat eggs and dairy products.

Vegans won't eat anything that originates from an animal, so that means no eggs, milk or cheese and if they're really strict, no honey, as that exploits bees.

Pritikin Diet is an American inspired healing diet, often recommended for people who are overweight or who have heart problems. It advocates reducing the amount of sugar, salt, oil, animal fats and caffeine, items that are all too prevalent in a Western diet. They do allow white meat and non-oily fish so are not vegetarians, but do include many vegetable dishes in their cooking.

Macrobiotic Diet is more than a diet, it's a whole philosophy of life, including food & cooking. Its basic premise is balancing the yin & yang – opposing forces eg acid/alkali; hot/cold. In practical terms the diet tends to consist of grains – rice, wheat, millet, barley – as the staple food with smaller amounts of vegetables, fruits and seeds. It is not necessarily a vegetarian diet, as fish & white meat are allowed. The aim is also to simplify food, use no artificial foodstuffs and where possible to use locally grown food. In practice, this is often difficult, as the diet originated in Japan where tamari, miso, seaweed, tofu and rice are common foods ~ these are now imported and easily available here. Attention is also paid to the methods of cooking, including the ways of cutting vegetables and the type of pots & utensils used.

Allergy Diets
~ these diets are not necessarily vegetarian, but we often get asked to provide dishes without milk or wheat and usually we have something on the menu for them.

Celiacs
are allergic to gluten, the protein part of many grains such as wheat & oats.

Dairy Allergies
~ dairy-food-free diets are often recommended for people with sinus troubles such as hay fever.

Some Mysteries Explained

"Miso is a...."

TAMARI ~ commonly known as soy sauce, tamari comes from Japan rather than China. It is a strong, good quality soy sauce, made of only natural products~ soya beans and salt, with no monosodium glutamate, sugar or colourings often found in cheaper soy sauces. Available from health shops, Chinese shops and some supermarkets.

TEMPEH ~ a member of the soya bean family, tempeh is of Indonesian origin. It is made from cultured soya beans compressed into a thin block. It has a strong flavour and retains its shape well in cooking. You'll find it only in health shops, and you may have to ask around to find your local supplier. For more information on tempeh, turn to page 133.

TOFU ~ yet another soya bean derivative. Tofu has a fragile texture and little taste, but is high in protein and easily digestible. You'll find it in little plastic trays in Chinese shops and some health shops. For further information, turn to page 122.

MISO ~ would you believe yet another product of the versatile soya bean. It is like a "tamari paste", with a slightly more subtle flavour. There are many different kinds, depending on which grains have been mixed with the beans ~ barley, wheat etc. We usually use hatcho or mugi miso. You'll find it in sealed plastic bags in health shops. Keep it in the fridge after opening.

TAHINI ~ not a member of the soya bean clan! Tahini is a sesame seed paste, (rather like smooth peanut paste) frequently used in Middle Eastern cooking. It is not usually emulsified, so remember to mix the oil layer into the paste before use. Tahini can be found in many Greek delis, and in health shops.

DRIED MUSHROOMS ~ we use Chinese dried mushrooms in some of our dishes. Look for the ones that have a normal mushroom shape but with a dark brown top and cream gills. Soak the mushrooms in boiling water for 20 mins before use, and discard the stalks as they are extremely tough. Available from Chinese shops and some good delis; they are rather expensive but a little goes a long way, and they do have a very distinctive flavour not found in ordinary mushrooms.

NORI ~ is a seaweed, usually found processed into thin, paper-like sheets which need no further cooking. Available from health shops and Japanese shops.

HEJIKI ~ is another sort of seaweed, looking like curly strands of hair. Available from health shops or Japanese shops.

PLUM SAUCE ~ a hot, spicy, jam-like savoury sauce used in Japanese and Chinese dishes, and can be used as a dip. Found in Chinese shops.

NUTTELEX ~ the brand name of a margarine made of vegetable oils, but without any milk products, so it is useful for vegan dishes. You can substitute butter or ordinary vegetable oil margarines. Nuttelex is available from health shops.

FILO PASTRY ~ is a paper thin sheet of pastry, made from flour and water. When brushed with butter, layered and baked, it produces light, flaky, mouth-watering delicacies. It's much easier to buy it ready made, and you'll find it in most Greek shops, delis and even the occasional supermarket.

AND A FEW MORE....!

<u>MIRRIN</u> ~ Japanese sherry.
<u>KOMBU</u> ~ seaweed - find it in a Japanese shop too.
<u>AGAR AGAR</u> ~ seaweed again, but Indian.
<u>GLUTEN</u> ~ wheat protein.
<u>TORULA YEAST</u> ~ non-dairy yeast.
<u>COUS COUS</u> ~ Moroccan grain - related to wheat.

SOUPS & STARTERS

Miso & Green Vegetable Soup

1 medium onion, chopped
1 tsp grated fresh ginger
1 stalk fresh lemon grass
2 sticks kombu seaweed
1 tsp garlic, crushed
½ tsp caraway seeds
1 tbs good miso Eg sorba

6 cups water
1 cup mixed carrots & zucchinis cut in thin 'julienne' (matchsticks)
½ cup mixed broccoli & cauliflower cut in thin slices

▽ To make the stock, put the onion, ginger, garlic, lemon grass, kombu, caraway, miso and water into a pan, bring to the boil and simmer for 20 mins.
▽ Strain the broth, then add the carrots, zucchinis, broccoli and cauliflower.
▽ Simmer for 5 mins then serve piping hot.

SPLIT PEA SOUP

250 g green or yellow split peas
1 large onion, finely chopped
2 cloves garlic, crushed
1 carrot, finely chopped
2 tbs oil
3 cups water
Salt & pepper
Pinch of thyme & a bay leaf

✡ Soak the split peas in the water for an hour or two. Then bring them to the boil and simmer for ½ hr until tender and soupy.

✡ Heat the oil in a frying pan and fry the onions, garlic and carrots over a moderate heat for 5 mins.

✡ Add the fried vegetables to the split peas, with the herbs and season well with salt and pepper.

✡ Simmer for a further 15 mins, adding more water if necessary.

✡ The soup can be served as it is or it can be pureed in a blender until smooth.

Curried Cauliflower Soup

2 onions
Small piece Ginger
3 cloves garlic
1 cauliflower
1 tsp curry paste
2 tbs oil
1 can coconut milk
1 tsp each of turmeric, paprika, coriander, cumin, poppy seeds & mustard seeds
Salt & pepper

- Finely chop the onions, garlic and ginger, put them in a saucepan with the oil and fry gently for 5 mins.
- Add the spices and fry a further 2 mins.
- Roughly chop the cauliflower and add to the pan, stir-fry for 2 mins.
- Add the coconut milk, and just enough water or stock to barely cover the cauliflower.
- Season well, then cover and simmer for ½ hr.
- Whiz the soup in a blender until smooth, return to the pot and reheat.
- Serve the soup with a spoonful of yoghurt and a sprinkle of fresh chopped coriander or parsley.

MINESTRONE

2 tbs olive oil
1 large onion, chopped
2 cloves garlic, crushed
1 large carrot, small dice
2 sticks celery, small dice
100g green beans, sliced
4 large tomatoes, chopped

100g haricot beans
100g wholemeal macaroni
1 x 140g tin tomato paste
1½ litres stock or water
1 tsp basil
1 tsp oregano
Salt & pepper

- Soak the haricot beans for a few hours or overnight. Simmer for 30 mins or until tender but not mushy.
- Heat the olive oil and add the onions, garlic, celery, carrot and beans. Fry for 10 mins until turning brown.
- Add the basil + oregano, then the tomatoes & fry for 5 mins.
- Add the remaining ingredients, season well and simmer for ½ hr. Stir occasionally, and add more water if the soup gets too thick.
- Serve with plenty of fresh Parmesan cheese and garlic bread.

CAULI-BROCCOLI SOUP

¼ cup olive oil
2 medium onions, chopped
3 cloves garlic, crushed
3 tbs wholemeal flour

2 tbs tamari
1½ litres stock or water
1 kg broccoli & cauliflower, mixed & chopped

- Heat the oil in a pan and fry the onions & garlic over a moderate heat for 10 mins or so, until they are going quite brown.
- Add the flour and continue to fry, stirring all the time, until the flour begins to brown.
- Pour in the stock & tamari, and add the broccoli and cauliflower pieces.
- Simmer the soup for ½ hr, then whizz in a blender until smooth. Check the seasoning, and serve garnished with a sprig of parsley and some hot herb bread.

ZUCCHINI & DILL SOUP

1 kg. zucchinis
1 tbs. chopped fresh dill
1 large onion, chopped
2 tbs Nuttelex

½ cup of cream or soya milk
salt & pepper
stock or water

- Chop or slice the zucchinis
- Melt the Nuttelex, add the chopped onion and sauté for 5 mins. until just turning brown.
- Add the zucchinis and enough water to barely cover the veggies.
- Simmer for ½ hr. until the zucchinis are soft.
- Puree in a processor or blender, then add the cream or soya milk and season well.

Leek & Potato Soup

4 leeks, sliced in rounds
25g. Nuttelex
2 cups diced raw potato
500mls. dashi or vecon
(vegetarian stock)
1 cup soya milk

- Melt the Nuttelex in a large saucepan and add the leeks.
- Fry gently for about 5 mins. — but don't brown them.
- Add the potatoes and fry for 2 mins., then add the stock and simmer for ½ hr.
- Sieve or blend the soup, and just before serving, add the soya milk.
- Sprinkle each serve with paprika or chopped parsley.

HUNGARIAN MUSHROOM SOUP

1 medium onion, chopped
1 tsp paprika
2 cups sliced mushrooms
2 cups stock
2 tbs butter

A good dash of white vinegar
1 cup cream
1 tbs unbleached white flour
Salt & pepper.

- Melt the butter in a pan and sauté the onions for 5 mins. Add the paprika and cook a minute more.
- Add the mushrooms and fry for a further 5 mins until the juices begin to run.
- Add the stock and vinegar and simmer for 20 mins.
- Mix the flour and cream together until smooth, whisk into the soup, then remove from the heat.
- Whiz in a blender until smooth, season with salt and pepper and serve piping hot.

Triple Mushroom Soup

6 dried Chinese mushrooms
1 x 250g can sliced champignons
250g fresh mushrooms, sliced
1 large onion, finely chopped
1 clove garlic, crushed
25g butter
25g plain wholewheat flour
1 litre stock or water
250 mls milk
3 tbs dry sherry
2 tbs tamari
Salt & pepper

- Boil 250mls of the water and soak the dried mushrooms for 20 mins. Drain and keep the liquid, remove the stalks and slice the mushrooms thinly.
- Heat the butter in a large pan and fry the onions and garlic for 5 mins. Add the fresh mushrooms, fry another 5 mins.
- Add the flour and gradually add the stock, milk and mushroom water; season with tamari, dry sherry, salt and pepper.
- Add the chinese mushrooms and champignons and simmer gently for ½ hr.
- Serve with a swirl of cream and some chopped shallots.

Corn Chowder

500g potatoes, cubed
1 large onion, chopped
250g sweetcorn ~
    fresh or frozen
500g mls milk
50g butter
250 mls stock or
    water
Pinch of nutmeg
A bayleaf
Salt & pepper

* Melt the butter in a large pan, add the onion and potato, and fry gently for 5 mins, stirring often.
* Add milk and stock, salt, pepper, nutmeg & bayleaf and simmer for 30 mins, stirring occasionally.
* Remove from heat, fish out the bayleaf and whiz the soup in a blender until smooth.
* Return to the heat, add sweetcorn and simmer for 10 mins.
* Check the seasoning, and if the soup is a little thick, add more milk or stock.
* Serve piping hot with a dollop of cream or sour cream and a sprinkle of parsley.

Hungarian Paprika Soup

2 carrots, diced
1 large potato, diced
1 large capsicum, diced
100g green beans, chopped
2 tbs oil
1 tbs paprika
2 bay leaves
4 cups stock or water
Salt & pepper

- Heat the oil in a large pan and fry all the vegetables together for 10 mins over a moderate heat, stirring often.
- Add the paprika, fry 2 mins, then add bay leaves, stock and season to taste.
- Simmer for 20 mins until the vegetables are tender.
- Serve with dark rye or pumpernickel bread and fresh butter.

Fresh Tomato and Zucchini Soup

1 kg ripe tomatoes, chopped
1 large onion, chopped
1 large clove garlic, crushed
4 tbs olive oil

250g zucchinis
Lots of fresh basil & oregano
or 1 tsp of each if using dried
Salt & pepper

- Heat 2 tbs oil in a large pan and fry the onions and garlic for 10 mins, gently. Add the tomatoes, herbs and salt and pepper, and about 1 cup water. Simmer for ½ hr.
- Meanwhile, slice the zucchinis thinly and fry them in the remaining 2 tbs olive oil for about 5 mins, until just begining to colour. Season, then set aside.
- Whiz the tomato soup in a blender until smooth, return to the pan, add the zucchinis and adjust the seasoning.
- Serve hot with lots of garlic bread.

CHINESE TOFU SOUP

150g tofu, in 1cm cubes
2 onions, thinly sliced
1 clove garlic, crushed
3 sticks celery, thinly sliced
100g snow peas, sliced
100g green beans, sliced
1 head broccoli, in florettes

3 tbs tamari
Pinch of aniseed
2 tbs dry sherry
1½ litres water
50g dried mushrooms
2 tbs oil
1 bunch watercress, chopped

- Soak the dried mushrooms in boiling water for 20 mins then slice thinly.
- Heat the oil in a pan and add the onions & garlic, fry for 2 mins.
- Add the celery, snow peas, broccoli & beans and stir fry for 5 mins, then add the sliced mushrooms.
- Mix together the tamari, aniseed, sherry, mushroom water and 1½ litres water and add to the soup. Simmer for 15 mins.
- Just before serving, add the tofu cubes and chopped watercress and heat through.

Guacamole

2 ripe avocados
1 ripe tomato, chopped
3 spring onions, sliced
juice of ½ lemon

3 tbs. sour cream
dash of tabasco sauce
salt and pepper

* Halve the avocados, remove the stones, and scoop out the flesh into a bowl.
* Mash the flesh well with the sour cream, lemon juice and tabasco.
* Mix in the tomato and onion, season well with salt and pepper - don't get too carried away in your tasting, or there'll be none left!
* Serve with corn chips or vegetable sticks.

TOFU CORIANDER BALLS

2 large cooked potatoes
250g. tofu
1 desertspoon soy sauce
1 bunch fresh coriander, finely chopped
cornflour, if required

For coating
sesame seeds
besan flour

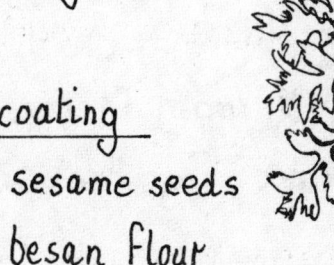

- Grate the potatoes, a dry type of potato is best.
- Crumble the tofu.
- Mix together with soy sauce and coriander.
- Make into balls; if mixture is too wet, add a little cornflour.
- Coat balls with a mixture of even parts of sesame seeds and besan.
- Deep fry until golden brown.

SERVE WITH SWEET AND SOUR SAUCE

Mushroom Pâté

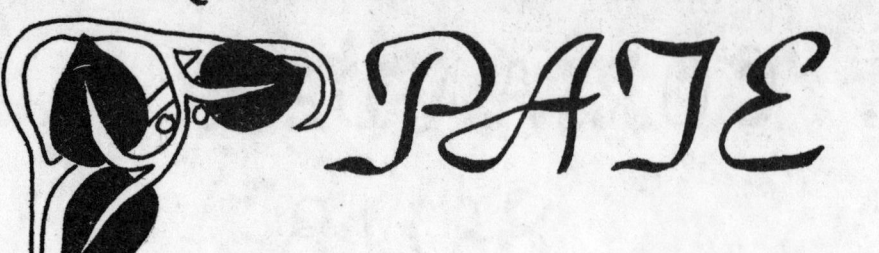

200g cream cheese
200g mushrooms, sliced
1 small onion, finely chopped
1 clove garlic, crushed

25g butter
2 tbs sherry, dry for preference
Fresh basil and tarragon
Salt & pepper

- Bring the cheese to room temperature.
- Melt the butter and fry the onions and garlic for 3 mins.
- Add the mushrooms and fry briskly for 2 mins. Add the basil and sherry and simmer 2 mins. Remove from the heat.
- Whiz in a food processor until finely chopped, then beat in the cream cheese. Season well with salt & pepper.
- Chill the pâté well before serving with fresh wholewheat bread, crackers or crispbreads.

Hummus

1 cup very well cooked chick peas
¼ cup tahini
½ cup olive oil
1 cup lemon juice
3 cloves garlic
salt

- Crush the garlic into a teaspoon of salt.
- Put the garlic, salt, chick peas and tahini in a processor and whiz together.
- Gradually add the lemon juice alternately with the olive oil and whiz until smooth.
- Taste to see if more salt is needed.
- Serve with chopped parsley and olive oil or sprinkled with paprika, with plenty of wholemeal pita bread and juicy olives.

Broad Bean Paté

500g. fresh or frozen broad beans
100g. cream cheese or soya cream
2 tbs. chopped parsley
2 tbs. lemon juice
salt & pepper

- You really do need a processor for this recipe.
- First, steam the broad beans for 10 mins, until tender, then cool them. Whiz them in a processor until smooth.
- Work the cream cheese, or soya cream, with a wooden spoon, and blend in the beans, along with parsley, lemon juice, salt & pepper.
- Chill the pate well, and serve with fresh homemade bread or sesame crackers.

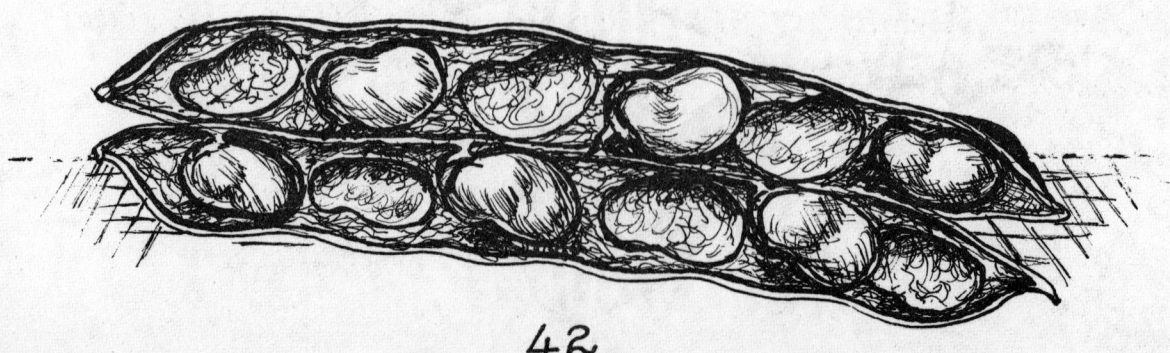

MUSHROOM BROCHETTE

For 4 people you'll need
24 medium mushrooms
1 red & 1 green capsicum
2 cups cooked rice
Oil for brushing   6 wooden skewers
The marinade ~
¼ cup dry sherry, ½ cup tamari, 1 tsp honey,   2 cloves garlic, crushed, 1 knob ginger, grated, 2 spring onions, chopped.

! Mix together all the ingredients for the marinade and soak the mushrooms for 2 hours.
! Cut the capsicums into 12 pieces each.
! Drain the mushrooms but reserve the marinade.
! Onto each wooden skewer, thread 6 mushrooms alternately with the red and green capsicums.
! Brochellc brochettes with oil and grill until sizzling or bake at 200°C for 10-15 mins.
! Serve them hot on a bed of rice, with a small bowl of the marinade on each plate to dip the mushrooms into.

TOSTADAS

250g cooked red kidney beans
1 onion, chopped
1 clove garlic, crushed
1 small piece ginger, grated
2 tbs olive oil
2 tsp cumin powder
½ tsp chilli powder
2 tbs tomato paste
100g grated cheese

Salt & pepper
6 tbs sour cream
Shredded lettuce
Bean shoots or alfalfa sprouts
Chilli sauce
Black olives
6 tortillas

- Heat the oil in a frying pan and sauté the onions, garlic and ginger for 5 mins. Add the cumin and chilli, fry for 2 mins then add the tomato paste, ½ cup water and the beans. Simmer for 10 mins, season well, then remove from the heat. Roughly mash the beans or whiz for a few seconds in a food processor.
- Cover the tortilla shells with the bean mixture, sprinkle with grated cheese and bake at 200°C for 10-15 mins until sizzling.
- To serve, top each tostada with a spoonful of sour cream, a dollop of chilli sauce, a handful of lettuce and sprouts, and an olive.

WANTED DEAD OR ALIVE
REWARD $200
For stealing 6 tostadas from Squirrels Restaurant

Russian Tartlets

200g mushrooms, thinly sliced
2 tbs butter
1 tbs fresh dill, chopped
A pinch of tarragon
3 tbs dry sherry
1 tsp horseradish sauce
1 tsp french mustard
250g carton sour cream
Salt and pepper
For the pastry –
150g plain wholewheat flour
75g margarine
Water to mix

- First make the pastry – rub the margarine into the flour and add just enough water to bind. Roll out the pastry fairly thin and cut out rounds to fit small patty tins.
- Bake the pastry cases for 5-7 mins at 200°C. When cooked, remove from the tins and place on a flat baking tray.
- For the filling, melt the butter in a pan and fry the mushrooms briskly until wilted and browning. Add the herbs and sherry and simmer until only half the liquid remains. Remove from the heat.
- Mix together the mushrooms, sour cream, horseradish and mustard, season well and place spoonfuls in each pastry case. Reheat the tartlets at 180°C for 5-10 mins and serve hot, garnished with a sprig of dill.

SPRING ROLLS

250g bean shoots
1 small can water-
    chestnuts, drained
50g mushrooms
½ capsicum

4 spring onions
1 small carrot
1 clove garlic, crushed
1 small piece fresh
    ginger, grated

3 tbs tamari
2 tbs dry sherry
1 packet spring
    roll wrappers
1 jar plum sauce

◁ Thinly slice the mushrooms and shred the carrot and capsicum.

◁ Combine all the vegetables, garlic and ginger, pour over the tamari and sherry, mix well and leave to marinade for ½ hr.

◁ Drain off the liquid and place small handfuls in one corner of a wrapper and roll up, tucking in the sides. Seal the last corner with a dab of water.

◁ Fry the rolls in deep or shallow oil until golden and crispy. Drain well and serve with plum sauce to dip into.

Stuffed Vine Leaves

½ pkt vine leaves
250g. cooked brown rice
1 onion, finely chopped
1 clove garlic, crushed
½ lemon, juice & rind plus
    2 slices
2 tbs. olive oil
25g. pinenuts or Sunflower seeds
2 tbs. chopped fresh parsley
1 tbs chopped fresh mint
250 mls. tomato juice
salt & pepper
2 tomatoes, finely chopped

- Heat the olive oil & toss in the onion & garlic. Fry for 5mins over a moderate heat. Add the tomatoes, parsley & mint and fry for 5mins. more. Cool.
- Mix together the tomato mixture, rice, pinenuts or sunflower seeds, lemon juice & rind, season well with salt & pepper.
- Rinse the vine leaves well, and roll 1 or 2 tbs. mixture in each leaf, tucking in the edges to make a neat parcel.
- Pack tightly together in a saucepan. Pour over the tomato juice and throw in the 2 slices of lemon. Simmer for 20-30 mins. over gentle heat, with a tight fitting lid on.
- The stuffed vine leaves can be served hot or cold.

STUFFED MUSHROOMS

18 large flat or cup mushrooms
150 g. fresh brown breadcrumbs
1 dsp. Horseradish
1 clove garlic, finely chopped
1 lemon, rind & juice
salt & pepper

ALSO KNOWN AS VERY TIRED MUSHROOMS!

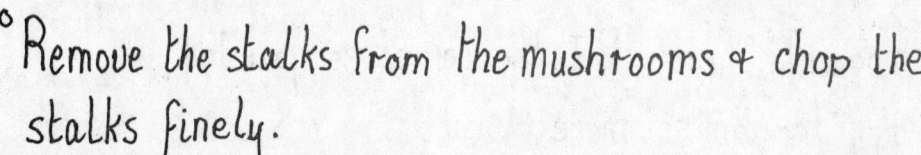

- Remove the stalks from the mushrooms & chop the stalks finely.
- Add breadcrumbs, lemon juice & rind, salt and pepper & Horseradish.
- Spoon the mixture into the mushroom caps.
- Place on an oiled tray, stuffed side up.
- Brush caps with a little margarine or Nuttelex.
- Bake for 10 mins at 200°c.

Gado Gado

✡ ✡ ✡ ✡ ✡ ✡

250g peanut butter
1 cup water
1 tin coconut milk
1 onion, finely chopped
1 clove garlic, crushed
1 small piece ginger, grated
1 tsp chilli powder or paste
1 tbs vinegar or lemon juice
1 tbs oil   2 tbs tamari

1 carrot
1 zucchini
1 small head broccoli
¼ head cauliflower
2 sticks celery
2 large handfuls fresh beanshoots
¼ lettuce, shredded

✡ Fry the onion, garlic & ginger gently together in the oil for 5 mins.

✡ Add the chilli and peanut butter, then the water and coconut milk, vinegar and tamari. Cook gently for 10 mins, adding more water if sauce gets to thick.

✡ Meanwhile, prepare the veggies ~ cut the carrot, celery & zucchini into thin sticks, and the broccoli and cauli in small florettes. Steam them together for 5 mins until just wilted. Allow to cool, then mix in the beanshoots.

✡ Arrange the lettuce on individual plates or bowls, place the veggies on top and pour over the sauce.

✡ Gado gado can be served as a main meal on a bed of rice ~ the veggies are usually cold and the sauce hot.

SAUCES AND DRESSINGS

SALADS & DRESSINGS

The two things that make the difference between an average salad and a super salad are the freshness of the vegetables, and the tastiness of the dressing. You should always remember to taste a dressing before pouring it over the salad — and remember that a small amount of dressing may have alot of veggies to cover, so to prevent it tasting bland, make sure it's extra tangy.

Here are some of our most popular dressings, and salads to show them off to best advantage......

VINAIGRETTE

- 2 tbs Olive oil
- 1 tbs Vegetable oil
- 2 tbs White vinegar
- 1 tbs Wine vinegar
- 1 tsp Dijon mustard
- A pinch of sugar
- 1 clove garlic
- Salt & pepper

○ If you have a food processor, whiz all the ingredients together for a few seconds.

○ If you don't, make sure the garlic is well crushed or chopped, then whisk all the ingredients together with a fork.

AVOCADO & LYCHEE

2 large ripe avocados
1 x 475g lychees, canned
1 clove garlic, chopped
1 tbs ginger, chopped
2 tbs tamari
2 tbs lemon juice

- Skin the avocados and cut into chunky pieces.
- Drain the juice from the lychees and add them to the avocado.
- Combine the tamari, lemon juice, garlic & ginger, and mix gently into the salad.

THOUSAND ISLAND

Thousand island dressing:-
1 qty mayonnaise
1 tbs tomato paste
1 tbs tomato chutney
1 tsp paprika
A pinch raw sugar

The veggies:-
½ pineapple, in chunks
3 sticks celery, sliced
1 large apple, in chunks
6 gherkins, chopped

- Mix all the ingredients for the dressing.
- Prepare all the veggies and mix in the dressing.

SOYA MAYONNAISE
(EGGLESS)

½ cup of soya milk
2 cups of vegetable oil
2 tsp. tamari
1 tbs of dijon mustard
1 tbs of cider vinegar

- Put the cold soya milk into a liquidisor and turn to high speed.
- Slowly dribble the oil into the centre top of the liquidisor.
- Continue until it becomes a thick white cream.
- Add the remaining ingredients.

SOYA SOUR CREAM

½ cup of soya milk.
2 cups of vegetable oil
2 tsp tamari
1 dsp. dijon mustard
1 tbs of lemon juice.

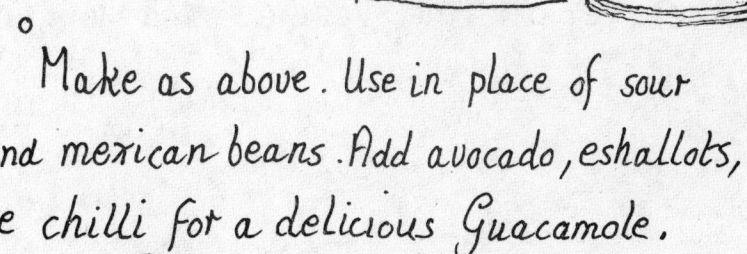

- Make as above. Use in place of sour cream in soup, and mexican beans. Add avocado, eshallots, chives, and a little chilli for a delicious Guacamole.

Tahini Sauce

½ cup tahini
¼ – ½ cup cold water
½ cup lemon juice

2 cloves garlic
salt

- Crush the garlic with ½ tsp salt and chop finely.
- Beat together the garlic & tahini.
- Gradually beat in the water and lemon juice alternately.
- Use all the lemon juice, and enough water to achieve the consistency you want.
- Check the seasoning, and serve.
- You can also use a food processor instead!

BARBECUE SAUCE

1 onion, finely chopped
1 clove garlic, crushed
1 small piece ginger, grated
2 tbs tomato paste
2 tbs Worcester sauce
2 tbs tamari
1 tbs oil
25g mushrooms, finely chopped
3 tbs crushed tinned pineapple
1 tbs brown vinegar
2 tbs cornflour
¼ tsp chilli

= Heat the oil in a pan, fry the onion, garlic & ginger gently for 5 mins. Add the mushrooms and fry a further 3 mins.
= Add the tomato paste, Worcester sauce, tamari, pineapple, vinegar, chilli and 1½ cups water, then simmer 15-20 mins.
= Mix the cornflour with ½ cup water to a smooth paste and stir briskly into the sauce; heat until thickened and bubbling ~ add a little more water if it's too thick.
= Check the seasoning ~ add more tamari if desired.
= Serve piping hot with burgers or kebabs.

Fettucine & Tomato Sauce

3 tbs olive oil
1 large onion, chopped
2 cloves garlic, crushed
1 capsicum, diced
1 large zucchini, sliced
1 small eggplant, cubed
4 ripe tomatoes, chopped
1 x 140g can tomato paste

½ cup red wine
½ cup stock or water
1 tsp basil
1 tsp oregano
salt & pepper
1 cup grated Parmesan
250g wholemeal fettucine or spaghetti

- Heat the oil in a pan and fry the onions & garlic for 5 mins.
- Add the capsicum, zucchini, eggplant & herbs, & fry for 10 mins, stirring often.
- Add the tomatoes & paste, wine, water, and season well. Simmer the sauce for 20 mins, adding a little more water if needed.
- Meanwhile, cook the pasta in plenty of boiling water for 15-20 mins. Drain and rinse with hot water.
- Serve the tomato sauce over the fettucine and plenty of Parmesan to sprinkle on top.

Mushroom Sauce

2 cups mushrooms, sliced
1 onion, finely chopped
2 cloves garlic, crushed
2 tbs Nuttelex
½ bunch fresh sweet basil, chopped

1 tbs. tamari
¼ cup dry sherry
2 cups soya milk
cornflour to thicken (optional)
salt and pepper

- Melt the Nuttelex in a saucepan and sauté the onions and garlic for 2 mins.
- Add the mushrooms, cover the pan with a lid and simmer for 15 mins.
- Add the tamari, soya milk, sherry and basil, season to taste with pepper and salt.
- Thicken with a little cornflour if you prefer a thicker sauce.
- Serve with mushroom loaf, pasta or steamed vegetables.

SALADS

CARROT & GINGER

3 medium carrots
½ cup sultanas
½ cup walnuts
¼ cup coconut

3 tbs oil
1 tbs fresh ginger, grated
2 tbs lemon juice
Salt & pepper

o Grate the carrots on a coarse grater. Mix the carrots with the sultanas, coconut & walnuts.
o Mix together the oil, ginger and lemon juice, add a little salt & pepper and pour over salad.
o Toss well and leave to marinade for at least ½ hr before serving.

INDIAN

1 cucumber, peeled
3 medium tomatoes
½ onion
3 tbs vinegar

¼ tsp chilli powder or paste
1 tbs fresh coriander, chopped
Pinch of sugar
Salt & pepper

o Cut the cucumber into quarters lengthwise and slice thinly. Chop the tomatoes and thinly slice the onion.
o Whisk together the vinegar, chilli, coriander, sugar, salt & pepper. Pour over the vegetables and mix well.
o This salad is particularly nice with curries.

GREEK MELON

1 medium melon - rock or honey dew, cubed
3 tomatoes in thin wedges
1 cucumber, peeled & cubed
50g black olives

Juice of 1 lemon
2 tbs olive oil
1 tsp honey
1 tbs chopped fresh mint
Salt & pepper

- Prepare the melon & vegetables, and mix together with the olives.
- Whisk together the lemon juice, oil, honey, mint, salt & pepper and pour over the salad. Mix well.
- Chill the salad well before serving.

ARAME

¼ pkt Arame sea vegetable
2 carrots, in thin matchsticks
1 medium Japanese radish (daikon) in thin matchsticks
4 spring onions, chopped
50g beanshoots

2 tbs tamari
1½ tbs mirrin
1½ tbs rice vinegar
½ clove garlic, crushed
Small piece of ginger, grated

- Soak the arame in hot water for 15 mins, changing the water at least twice. Drain and allow to cool.
- Mix together the arame, carrot, radish, spring onion and beanshoots.
- Whisk together the tamari, mirrin, rice vinegar, garlic and ginger. Pour over salad, mix well and leave to marinade for an hour or so.

Potato Salad

600g. cooked potatoes
8 shallots
A handful of parsley, chopped

2 hard boiled eggs (optional)
4 gherkins or dill-pickled cucumbers
Soya mayonnaise

- Cut the spuds into chunky cubes, chop the shallots and gherkins, roughly chop the eggs.
- Mix all the ingredients into the dressing - if it's too thick, add a little water to the dressing to thin it down.

 # MUSHROOM

250g	mushrooms, sliced	6	shallots, finely chopped
½	cucumber, diced	A handful parsley, chopped	
1 green	capsicum, diced		
2 sticks	celery, diced	1 qty	vinaigrette dressing

- Prepare all the veggies and toss together in vinaigrette.

WHEAT

100g	wholewheat grains		1 can	sweetcorn, drained
1 small	carrot	⎫	50g	cashews, toasted
1 stick	celery	⎬ all chopped in small cubes	50g	sultanas
1 small	capsicum		1 qty	vinaigrette
½	cucumber			
1 large	tomato			
1 med.	apple			
1 med.	zucchini	⎭		

- Cook the wheat grains in plenty of water for 30 mins. Drain and cool.
- Mix grain and veggies and toss in vinaigrette.

Salads with their own personal dressings...

WALDORF

6 sticks celery
3 apples - red & green
100g walnuts

1 cup yoghurt
½ cup sour cream
salt & pepper

- Slice the celery thinly on the slant, cut the apples into bite size cubes.
- Lightly toast the walnuts under a grill or in the oven until golden and crunchy.
- Mix the yoghurt, cream and seasonings, then combine dressing with celery, apples and walnuts.
- For a tasty variation, crumble blue cheese into the dressing.

CUCUMBER

1 large cucumber, peeled & sliced
6 shallots, chopped
A handful mint, chopped
½ tsp cumin powder
½ tsp coriander powder
1 cup natural yoghurt
salt & pepper

- Mix all the ingredients and chill well before eating.

TABOULEH

2 bunches parsley, chopped
1 bunch mint, chopped
100g bulghar
2 small tomatoes, diced
4 shallots, chopped
1 qty vinaigrette

- Soak the bulghur in hot water for 20 mins. Drain and squeeze out excess water.
- Mix all the ingredients together in a small amount of vinaigrette.

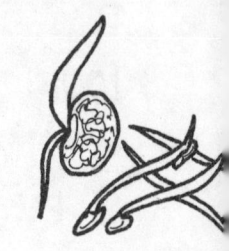

BEAN SPROUT

200g fresh white bean sprouts
1 carrot
1 zucchini
2 tomatoes
½ cucumber, peeled
2 sticks celery
1 capsicum
1 can sweetcorn, drained
1 small can sliced waterchestnuts
1 qty vinaigrette
50g red cabbage } optional
50g roasted peanuts

- Slice all the veggies into thin strips.
- Combine everything and toss in vinaigrette.

BROCCOLI & TOMATO

500g broccoli
250g tomatoes, cut in thin wedges
1 med. onion, thinly sliced
1 qty vinaigrette

- Cut the broccoli into mouth-sized florettes.
- Steam lightly for about 5 mins. Cool.
- Toss all the veggies together in vinaigrette.

SALAD NIÇOISE

1 small lettuce, in chunky pieces
200g cooked potatoes, cubed
½ cucumber, peeled & sliced
2 large tomatoes, in thin wedges
4 shallots, chopped
150g steamed green beans
3 hard boiled eggs
100g black and/or green olives
1 qty vinaigrette

- Prepare all the veggies and place together in a bowl.
- Separate the hard boiled eggs into yolks and whites.
- Roughly chop the whites and add them to the veggies.
- Whisk the yolks into the vinaigrette, and pour over the salad just before serving.

GREEK

1 small	lettuce, cut in chunky pieces
½	cucumber, peeled, halved lengthwise & sliced
3	tomatoes, cut in thin wedges
150g	feta cheese, cut in small cubes
1 med.	onion, cut in thin round slices
50g	black olives
1 q'ty	vinaigrette

Prepare all the ingredients and toss together in the vinaigrette. Serve soon or the lettuce will wilt.

GREEN BEAN

250g fresh green beans   1 med onion, chopped or sliced
4 med tomatoes, in thin wedges   1 q'ty vinaigrette

Top, tail and halve the beans. Steam them for 10mins, until just tender. Cool them, then mix with the remaining ingredients.

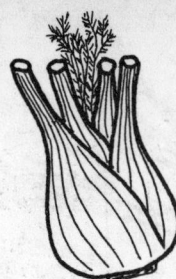 

ORANGE & FENNEL

1	lettuce, in chunky pieces	1	head fennel
3	oranges, peeled & sliced	2 sticks	celery, sliced
1	red capsicum, in thin rounds	1 tbs	poppy seeds
½	cucumber, peeled & sliced	1 qty	vinaigrette

- To prepare the fennel, cut the bulb in half lengthwise and remove the woody centre. Slice the rest of the bulb thinly.
- Whisk the poppy seeds into the vinaigrette.
- Mix all the veggies together and toss lightly in the dressing.

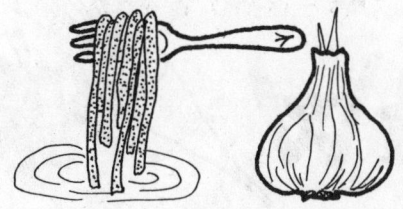 

PASTA

250g	cooked macaroni or fettucine	50g	black olives
1	zucchini, thinly sliced	6	shallots, chopped
2	tomato, thin wedges	1	capsicum, diced
½	cucumber, peeled & cubed	1 tbs	fresh oregano or basil
150g	cooked broccoli	1 qty	vinaigrette

- Prepare all the veggies and mix with the pasta.
- Finely chop the herbs, whisk into the vinaigrette, and smother the salad in the dressing. A very garlicky vinaigrette is good for this salad.

POTATO

500g	cooked potatoes	3	hard boiled eggs
6	shallots, chopped	A handful	parsley, chopped
6	gherkins, chopped	1 qty	mayonnaise

- We prefer to use our potatoes with their skins still on, so don't peel your potatoes, just boil or steam them until tender; cool and cut them into chunky cubes.

- Mix the potatoes with the remaining ingredients and gently stir in the mayonnaise. Chill well before eating.

COLESLAW

¼	cabbage, white &/or red	½	onion, chopped (optional)
1 med	carrot, coarsely grated	1 qty	mayonnaise
1 large	green apple, grated		salt, pepper & vinegar

- Shred the cabbage as finely as you can – use a really sharp knife to make this easier.

- Combine the cabbage, carrot, apple, onion and mayonnaise and add a little extra salt, pepper and vinegar for extra flavour.

TEMPEH & BEANSHOOT

Tamari marinade - dressing:-
- 3 tbs tamari
- 1 clove garlic, crushed
- 1 piece fresh root ginger, chopped
- 2 tbs malt vinegar
- 2 drops sesame oil

1 packet tempeh, cut in small diamonds

- 200g bean shoots
- 1 carrot
- 1 capsicum
- 2 tomatoes
- 1 zucchini
- 100g steamed green beans
- 1 small canned waterchestnuts
- 1 small canned bamboo shoots

- Mix all the ingredients for the marinade, and soak the tempeh in it for a few hours. Drain the tempeh, saving the marinade, and fry the tempeh in a little oil until golden. Cool.
- Chop the veggies into thin strips, add the tempeh and enough of the marinade to coat the salad, toss well and serve.

GREEN BEAN & ALMOND

- 200g steamed green beans
- 100g almonds
- 2 tbs tamari
- 1 clove garlic, crushed
- 1 tbs fresh root ginger, grated
- 1 large tomato, in thin wedges
- ½ med onion, thinly sliced
- 2 tbs oil

- Fry the almonds gently in a little oil, stirring frequently to prevent them burning. When golden, add the garlic, ginger and tamari. Cool.
- Mix the almonds with the veggies, toss well and serve.

STUFFINGS for VEGETABLES

Here are some ideas for vegetable stuffings ~ lots of veggies are suitable, so here's how to prepare them....

Eggplant ~ cut in half lengthwise, sprinkle with salt and leave for ½ hr. Rinse, brush with oil and put on an oiled tray. Bake at 180°C for 20-30 mins until soft. Scoop out the middle, but leave some flesh on the skin for support.

Capsicum ~ can be stuffed whole ~ just cut the tops off and remove the seeds. They will need 30-40 mins baking once stuffed. Or they can be halved lengthwise, and the seeds removed, in which case, they'll take about 20 mins in the oven.

Tomatoes ~ Slice off the top, and a little off the bottom if they are unstable, scoop out the pulp and use for a sauce. Bake for 15-20 mins, once filled.

Zucchinis ~ Choose larger, thicker ones, cut in half lengthwise and carve out a channel down the middle. They'll need baking 20-30 mins after stuffing.

Cabbage leaves ~ Choose fairly green leaves, remove whole and cut out the thickest part of the veins. Steam lightly for 4-5 mins to make them easier to roll up.

Pumpkins ~ you can use butternuts or small round nuggety ones. Either cut off the top, or split in half around the equator and scoop out the seeds. They will need pre-cooking ~ steaming or baking for about ½ hr before stuffing

Marrows ~ Cut into slices about 4cm wide, hollow out the centre and stuff. If old and tough, it's best to steam the slices for 10-15 mins before stuffing and baking for ½ hr or so.

Now for the stuffings.....
LEBANESE

50g burghul soaked in 250mls warm water
50g green lentils, cooked
1 large onion, chopped
1 clove garlic, crushed
50g mushrooms, chopped
1 large tomato, chopped
1 carrot, finely diced
2 sticks celery, finely diced
1 small capsicum, finely diced
1 egg
Good pinch of rosemary and oregano
Salt & pepper
A dash of tamari
3 tbs olive oil

- Heat the oil in a large frying pan and fry the onion and garlic for 5 mins.
- Add the carrot and celery, fry for another 5 mins ~ the veggies should be begining to brown.
- Add the capsicum and mushrooms and herbs, fry 2 mins then throw in the tomatoes, season well and fry a

further 5 mins. Remove from the heat.
- Mix in the cooked lentils; squeeze the water out of the burghul and add that along with the egg. Stir well and add a dash of tamari.
- Stuff the veggies with the mixture - it's particularly good with eggplant - add the scooped out pulp to the stuffing - and serve with a tomato or chasseur sauce.

INDONESIAN

100g brown rice, cooked
6 spring onions, sliced
1 clove garlic, crushed
Small piece of ginger, chopped
1 zucchini, diced
1 capsicum, diced
2 tbs vegetable oil

1 can water chestnuts
60g cashews, toasted
A handful of beanshoots
25g creamed coconut
¼ tsp chilli powder or paste
Tamari or sweet Indonesian soy sauce - ketchap Betang

- Heat the oil in a wok and fry the garlic and ginger, zucchini and capsicum together for 5 mins. Add the spring onions and fry a further 5 mins.
- Drain and chop the waterchestnuts, add them to the wok along with the beanshoots and creamed coconut, and heat until the coconut has melted; remove from heat.
- Add the chilli and soy sauce, mix into the rice, and stuff the vegetables. Bake and serve with a coconut or orange sauce.

ITALIAN

200g brown rice, cooked
1 bunch spinach or silverbeet
1 large onion, sliced
1 clove garlic, crushed
100g fresh Parmesan, grated
50g pinenuts
Salt & pepper
3 tbs olive oil

- Wash, drain and shred the spinach (discard the stalks).
- Heat the oil in a large frying pan and fry the onions and garlic gently, stirring often, until they begin to brown.
- Add the pinenuts and fry for 3 mins until just browning.
- Throw in the spinach, and cook for 5mins, until the spinach is wilted and tender. Remove from the heat.
- Add the rice and Parmesan, season well, and use to stuff the veggies ~ tomatoes are particularly tasty.
- Serve with a herby tomato sauce.

BRAZILIAN

100g Brazil nuts, toasted
100g brown rice, cooked
25g sunflower seeds
1 large onion, chopped
1 clove garlic, crushed
1 capsicum, chopped
2 tbs vegetable oil

1 carrot, finely diced
1 small tin sweetcorn, drained
Handful of green beans, chopped
Grated rind of 1 orange
1/4 tsp chilli powder
1/4 tsp coriander powder
Salt & pepper

- Heat the oil in a large frying pan and fry the onion and garlic for 5 mins. Add the carrot, capsicum and beans and fry gently until the veggies are tender. Add the chilli and coriander and fry for 30 secs. Remove from heat.

- Chop the brazil nuts and add them to the fried vegetables along with the sunflower seeds, rice and orange rind. Season well and stuff the vegetables. Bake and serve with an orange sauce.

OTHER IDEAS

Indian ~ stuff the veggies with a thick dhal (split peas with onions and spices), bake and serve with a yoghurt raita.

Mexican ~ stuff veggies with chilli bean mix ~ you can add a little cornmeal to thicken the sauce. Serve with a chilli or piquant sauce & decorate with corn chips.

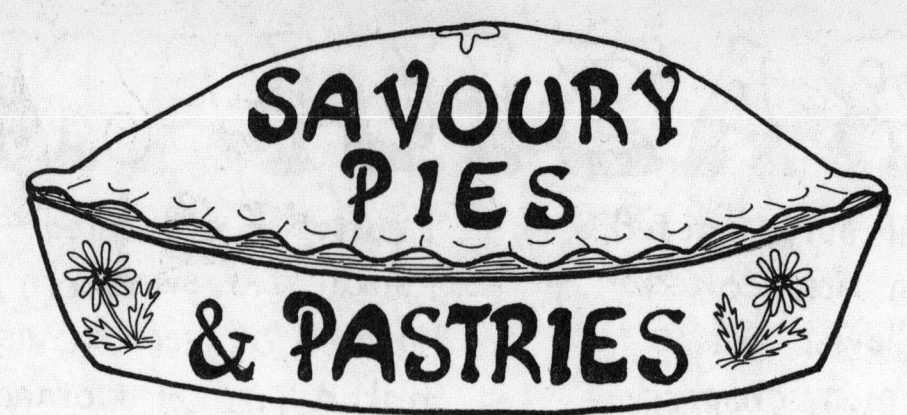

SAVOURY PIES & PASTRIES

Lots of people live in fear of pastry making, believing it to be a gift of the gods one either has or has not. But in fact it's easy if you follow a few basic rules:-

* The proportion of fat : flour should be 1:2 eg 250g margarine to 500g plain flour.
* Use cold water, and don't use too little. The water makes the pastry hold together, and if you don't use enough, your pastry will crumble to bits as you try to roll it. Also remember wholewheat flour tends to absorb more water than white flour.
* Don't over-handle the pastry. Once you have formed it into a ball with the correct amount of water, give it a light 5 second knead to smooth out cracks — but that's all, don't over-knead.
* When rolling out the pastry, make sure it doesn't stick to board or pin by using a good sprinkle of flour. Use light, short strokes to roll — don't pound or stretch the pastry.

To make 2 quiche bases or 1 closed pie......

250g plain wholewheat flour
125g vegetable oil margarine
½ - ¾ cup cold water
pinch of salt

* Rub the margarine into the flour, add the water and work into a ball. Divide dough in half, and roll each half separately to form the base and top of the pie.

Quiche Provençal

Half quantity of pastry
2 zucchinis, sliced
½ eggplant, in small cubes
1 capsicum, diced
2 tomato, diced
1 clove garlic, finely chopped
1 onion, chopped
2 tbs olive oil

½ tsp basil
½ tsp oregano
3 eggs
1 cup cream
100g cheddar or Gruyère cheese, grated
salt & pepper

* Line a quiche dish with the pastry
* Heat the olive oil in a frying pan and toss in the onions and garlic; fry for 5 mins.
* Add the capsicum, eggplant and zucchini and fry gently, stirring occasionally, until almost tender.
* Add the tomatoes, herbs, salt & pepper, and cook a further 2 mins.
* Cool, then pour into pastry base and sprinkle with cheese.
* Whisk the eggs and cream with a little salt & pepper and pour over the quiche.
* Bake at 180-200°C for 30-40 mins.

This is a slightly more hearty quiche, suitable for a deeper pie dish. You can substitute milk for all or part of the cream, if you wish.

Broccoli & Walnut Pie

Full quantity of pastry
300mls white sauce (p190)
1 head broccoli
100g walnuts
¼ cup cream
2 egg yolks

1 onion, chopped
25g butter
¼ tsp marjoram
salt & pepper
beaten egg to glaze

* Cut the broccoli into florets and steam for 7-10 mins until tender but crunchy still.

* Line a pie dish with half the pastry.

* Fry the onions in the butter over a gentle heat until just browning.

* Gently toast the walnuts under a grill or in the oven until crisp but not browning.

* Mix the walnuts, broccoli, onions, white sauce, cream, egg yolks, marjoram, salt & pepper. Pour into the pastry case.

* Roll out the remaining pastry and top the pie, seal and brush with egg. Make a small slit in the middle.

* Bake for 20-30 mins at 200°C until golden brown.

SPINACH & RICOTTA PIE

Full quantity of pastry
1 bunch spinach or silver beet
500g Ricotta cheese
100g Fresh grated Parmesan

salt & pepper
¼ tsp nutmeg
beaten egg to glaze
poppy seeds

* Line a pie dish with half the pastry mix.
* Remove stalks from spinach, then steam the leaves for 5 mins until just tender. Drain well, then chop roughly.
* Mix the ricotta, parmesan, spinach and seasonings.
* Pour into the prepared pastry case. Roll out remaining pastry to cover the pie; seal and trim the edges.
* Make a small slit in the pastry top, then brush with beaten egg and sprinkle with poppy seeds.
* Bake at 200°C for 20-30 mins until golden brown.

gnocchi

3 cups water
2/3 cup semolina or cornmeal
1 tsp. salt
pinch nutmeg & pepper
50g. Nuttelex
100g. parmesan cheese

2 tbs. olive oil
1 small fine chopped onion
1 clove garlic, crushed
1 small can tomato paste
½ tsp. each oregano & basil
Salt & pepper

- Heat the water, salt, pepper & nutmeg in a pan until boiling.
- Throw in the semolina and stir rapidly until smooth. Cook for 5 mins until very thick.
- Remove from heat, beat in ½ the parmesan, then pour onto an oiled tray to 1½cm. thickness. Allow to cool and set.
- Cut out rounds of the gnocchi and place in an oiled baking dish, pour over melted Nuttelex & remaining parmesan. Bake at 200°c. for 15-20 minutes.
- Serve with tomato sauce ~ fry the onion and garlic 5 mins. add the herbs, tomato paste & seasonings, and enough water to make a good sauce. Simmer for 15 mins. and serve in a separate sauce boat.
- This dish makes a good starter or main meal.

IRISH STEW with POTATO DUMPLINGS

The Stew~
- 50g haricot beans
- 1 potato, cubed
- 1 carrot, sliced
- 1 small turnip, cubed
- 1 parsnip, sliced
- 2 sticks celery, sliced
- 1 large onion, chopped
- 1 leek, sliced
- 50g butter
- 100mls Guinness
- 1 tbs Vegemite
- 2 bay leaves
- Good pinch of mixed herbs. Salt & pepper

The Dumplings~
- 100g S.R. wholemeal flour
- 2 cooked potatoes
- 1 tsp baking powder
- 25g butter
- 1 egg
- 2 tbs yoghurt
- Milk to mix
- Pinch of nutmeg, salt & pepper

- Soak the beans overnight in plenty of water, then cook until tender.
- Melt the butter in a large pot, add the onions and leeks, sauté gently for 3 mins. Add the rest of the vegetables and sauté for 10 mins, stirring often.
- Add the herbs, bay leaves, Vegemite and Guinness, season well, and top up with enough water, stock or bean cooking liquid to barely cover the veggies. Simmer gently for 20 mins until the veggies are just tender. Add the cooked beans.
- Meanwhile, make the dumplings~ mash the potatoes, mix in the flour and butter and baking powder, salt & pepper & nutmeg. Whisk the egg & yoghurt with a little milk, and add to potato mix to form a dough.
- Roll dough into small balls and pop on top of stew. Cover with a lid and steam gently for 20 mins ~ or put stew & dumplings in a baking dish and bake at 180°C for 20-30 mins.

PIZZA PIZZA PIZZA

The Base –
- 250g wholemeal flour
- 15g fresh yeast
- ½ tsp salt
- 1 tbs oil
- ¾ – 1 cup warm water

The Top –
- 1 tbs olive oil
- 1 onion, fine chopped
- 2 cloves garlic, crushed
- 400g can chopped tomatoes
- 2 tbs tomato paste
- ½ tsp each basil & oregano
- 150g Cheddar or Mozzarella cheese

- ☐ Dissolve the yeast in some of the water. Mix the flour & salt in a bowl, pour in the yeast, oil and enough water to make a dough. Knead for 2 mins until smooth & elastic. Put back in the bowl, cover, and leave to rise for 20 mins.
- ☐ Meanwhile, prepare the sauce – fry the onions & garlic for 5 mins, add the herbs, tomatoes and paste, season well and simmer for 10 mins.
- ☐ Roll out the dough to line a round or square oiled baking tray.
- ☐ Pour the tomato sauce over the dough, and sprinkle with grated cheese – Cheddar tastes better but Mozzarella is more authentic.
- ☐ Bake the pizza at 220°C for 15-20 mins until crisp and golden. Serve with a crisp, garlicky green salad.
- ☐ If you don't fancy making the dough, use wholemeal pita or flat bread instead as a base.

SOYARONI MARINARIA

5 tbs olive oil
50g butter
1 capsicum, sliced
3 cloves garlic, crushed
2 tbs capers, chopped

100g chopped black olives
350g can crushed tomato
½ cup grated carrot
½ cup tomato paste
½ cup sherry

1 tsp oregano
½ ts thyme
¼ pkt hejiki seaweed
400g soyaroni
salt & pepper

- Heat the oil & butter in a pan and saute the garlic and capsicum until just begining to colour.
- Add the capers, olives, crushed tomato and grated carrot and simmer gently for 15 mins.
- Add the tomato paste, sherry and hejiki & herbs, season well and cook for a further 15 mins.
- Meanwhile, cook the soyaroni in plenty of boiling water for 10-15 mins. When tender, drain and stir gently into sauce.
- Serve the dish sprinkled with fresh grated parmesan.
- For variety, try adding ½ chopped chilli pepper to the sauce.
- The dish can easily be made vegan by omitting the butter and parmesan - use toasted pinenuts as a garnish instead.

LASAGNE

- 6 sheets lasagne
- 1 onion
- 2 cloves garlic
- 1 capsicum
- 1 stick celery
- 1 zucchini
- 1 small eggplant
- 3 small tomatoes
- 1 carrot
- 135ml can tomato paste
- 1 tsp basil
- 1 tsp oregano
- ¼ cup red wine
- ½ cup water or stock
- 3 tbs olive oil
- salt & pepper
- 1 tbs margarine
- 1 tbs plain wholemeal flour
- 250 mls milk
- 50g grated cheddar cheese
- 25g grated Parmesan cheese

- Boil a big pot of water with 1 tbs oil and add the lasagne sheets one at a time. Boil for 20 mins, stirring often to prevent sticking. Drain and leave sheets in cold water.
- Chop all the veggies into 1cm dice. Heat the olive oil in a large pan and toss in the onions and garlic, fry 5 mins.
- Add the capsicum, carrot, celery, zucchini & eggplant and fry for 10 mins, then add the herbs, tomato & paste, wine, stock and seasonings. Simmer for 20 mins until the veggies are tender.
- Meanwhile make a cheese sauce - melt the margarine, stir in the flour, gradually add the milk and stir until thickened. Add the cheddar cheese, salt & pepper
- To assemble - take a deep casserole. Put a layer of tomato sauce in the bottom, then a layer of lasagne, a layer of tomato, lasagne and so on until all is used. Pour over the cheese sauce, sprinkle with Parmesan and bake at 180°C for ½ hr.

TOFU & Mushroom on Spinach Pasta

500g. tofu, cubed
1 cup sliced mushrooms
1 cup quartered mushrooms
2 tbs. tamari
2 cloves garlic, crushed
1 small onion, chopped
1 x 75g. can green peppercorns
1 bunch shredded spinach or silverbeet
1 cup soya milk
1 cup stock
¼ cup dry sherry
2 tbs. corn flour
¼ cup water
250g. spinach noodles
2 tbs. Nuttelex

" Melt the Nuttelex in a pan, add the onions & garlic and fry 5min.
" Add the sliced mushrooms and fry a further 5mins.
" Now add the quartered mushrooms, tamari, sherry, stock & peppercorns, heat gently until almost boiling.
" Mix the cornflour & water and stir into the sauce, heat until thickened, and simmer for 5mins., then add the soya milk, tofu & shredded spinach and check the seasoning.
" Boil the pasta for 10-15mins. in plenty of water, drain well, and serve the sauce over the pasta.

Caterina's Cannelloni

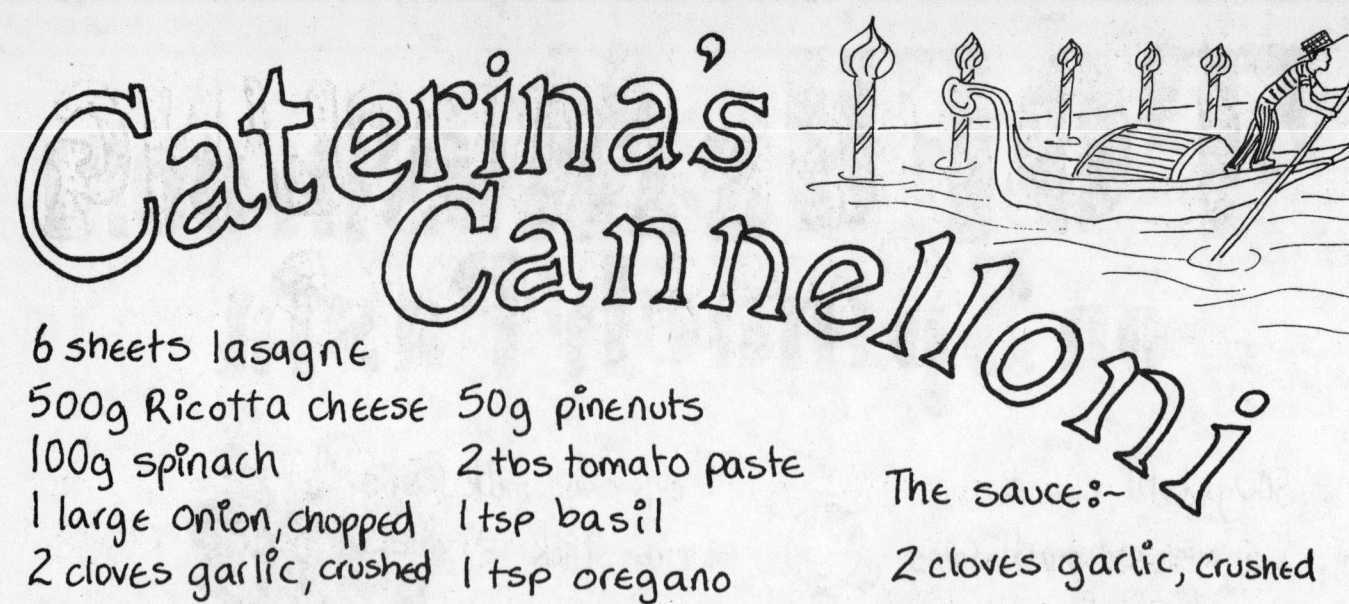

6 sheets lasagne
500g Ricotta cheese
100g spinach
1 large onion, chopped
2 cloves garlic, crushed
3 ripe tomatoes, chopped
2 tbs olive oil

50g pinenuts
2 tbs tomato paste
1 tsp basil
1 tsp oregano
Salt & pepper
50g Parmesan cheese

The sauce:-

2 cloves garlic, crushed
500g ripe tomatoes
Basil & oregano

- Cook the lasagne in plenty of water. Rinse and leave in cold water.
- Steam the spinach for 3 mins, then chop finely.
- Heat the olive oil in a frying pan and saute the onion & garlic together for 5 mins. Add the pinenuts, & herbs, saute 2 mins, then add the chopped tomatoes, simmer for 15 mins.
- Mix together the ricotta, spinach, tomato mixture and tomato paste, season well with salt & pepper, set aside to cool.
- Next prepare the sauce — chop the tomatoes and put them in a pan with 1 tbs olive oil, the garlic, herbs to taste, salt & pepper. Stew for 20 mins, then puree in a blender.
- To make the Cannelloni, take a sheet of lasagne, cut it in half width-wise, place a good spoonful of mixture along one edge, then roll up. Place the rolls in an oiled baking dish.
- When all the sheets are completed, pour over the tomato sauce, sprinkle with grated parmesan, and bake at 180°C for 30 mins until golden and sizzling.

Cheese Dumpling Casserole

4 good size zucchinis
2 onions, sliced,
2 cloves garlic, crushed
6 large ripe tomatoes
½ tsp oregano
 salt & pepper
3 tbs olive oil

200g bakers cheese
50g grated cheddar cheese
75g brown bread crumbs
1 egg
A pinch of thyme & nutmeg

- Slice the zucchinis in thin slices, the tomatoes into thin wedges. Heat the oil in a big pan and fry the onions and garlic for 5 mins. Add the zucchinis and fry a further 5 mins, then add the tomatoes, oregano, salt & pepper and simmer together for 15 mins.
- Combine the cheeses, breadcrumbs, herbs, egg and salt & pepper and form into small dumplings.
- Pour the zucchini & tomato mixture into a shallow casserole and arrange the dumplings on top.
- Bake at 180°C for 20-30 mins until the dumplings are browning and the casserole bubbling.

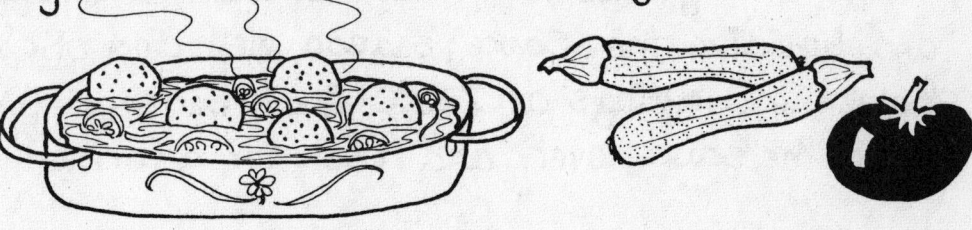

Eggplant Dumplings

2 medium eggplants, peeled
1 capsicum, finely chopped
1 onion, finely chopped
1 clove garlic, crushed
2 tbs water
100g soya grits
100g grated Cheddar cheese
100g wholemeal breadcrumbs
1 egg
Salt & pepper

For the sauce:-
1 carrot, chopped
1 onion, chopped
2 tbs oil
2 tbs plain wholemeal flour
2 cups stock or water with 1 tbs Vegemite
¼ cup cream
2 bay leaves
Salt & pepper

- Cut the eggplant into small cubes. Sprinkle with salt, leave 20 mins, rinse, drain & dry. Heat the oil and fry the eggplant for 10 mins until soft. Remove from the pan & set aside.
- Add the onion, garlic & capsicum to the pan & fry for 5 mins, then add the soya grits & water and cook for a further 5 mins; add more water if it begins to burn or stick. Cool.
- Mix together all the dumpling ingredients and form into balls. Lay in an oiled casserole.
- Next, make the sauce ~ fry the carrot & onion very slowly for 20 mins until golden brown. Add the flour and stir in the stock. Add the bay leaves & simmer for 20 mins. Remove the bay leaves and liquidize the sauce; season well and stir in the cream.
- Bake the dumplings at 200°C for 10 mins on their own, then pour the sauce over and cook for a further 10-15 mins.

MOUSSAKA

- 2 eggplant, large size
- 1 onion
- 2 cloves garlic, crushed
- 1 large carrot
- 2 zucchinis
- 1 capsicum
- 3 tbs tomato paste
- 400g can tomatoes
- 100g cooked chick peas
- Good pinch each of basil, oregano & rosemary
- 2 tbs margarine
- 2 tbs plain flour
- 300 mls milk
- 200g grated cheese
- salt & pepper
- oil for frying

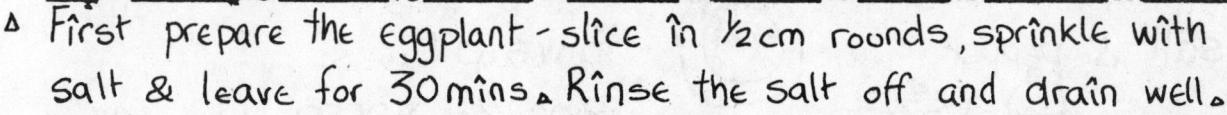

- First prepare the eggplant - slice in ½cm rounds, sprinkle with salt & leave for 30 mins. Rinse the salt off and drain well.
- Heat 1cm depth oil in a heavy frying pan and fry the eggplant slices, a few at a time, for 3 mins each side, until golden. Drain on kitchen paper.
- Cut the veggies into 1cm dice. Heat a little oil in a pan & fry the onions & garlic together for 3 mins, add the carrot, capsicum & zucchini. Fry for 5 mins, then add the tomatoes & paste, herbs and a little water and simmer for about 15 mins until tender.
- Season well and set aside. Mash the chick peas & add to sauce.
- Next the sauce - melt the margarine in a pan, add the flour then gradually stir in the milk and cook slowly until thick and smooth; add salt & pepper to taste.
- To assemble - place half the eggplant slices in the bottom of a casserole. Pour over the tomato-chickpea sauce and cover with remaining eggplant. Pour over white sauce and sprinkle with cheese.
- Bake at 180-200°C for ½ hr until golden & bubbling.

ZUCCHINI BASED PIZZA

mama mia!

The Base ~
- 4 cups finely grated zucchini
- ½ cup plain wholemeal flour
- ½ cup grated Mozzarella
- 3 eggs
- ½ tsp basil
- salt & pepper

The Top ~
- 1 onion, chopped
- 2 cloves garlic, crushed
- 1 x 500g tin tomatoes
- 3 tbs tomato paste
- ½ tsp each basil & oregano
- olive oil
- 200g grated Cheddar cheese

- Combine all the ingredients for the base, mix well, and press into a well greased shallow dish. Bake at 180°C for 20 mins.

- Meanwhile, make the pizza sauce ~ heat 2 tbs olive oil in a frying pan, and fry the onions & garlic for 5 mins. Add ther herbs, tomatoes & paste, season well and simmer for 15 mins.

- Pour the tomato sauce over the baked zucchini base, sprinkle with grated cheddar cheese, and finish baking at 200°C for about 15 mins until the cheese is turning golden.

Pumpkin Souffle

1 kg pumpkin
1 cup sour cream
100g feta cheese
100g grated Cheddar cheese

½ cup chopped shallots
3 eggs
Salt & pepper

- Peel and remove the seeds from the pumpkin, and steam or boil for 20-30 mins until soft. Cool and drain.
- Mash the pumpkin well, then mix in the feta, cheddar, sour cream, shallots, salt & pepper.
- Separate the eggs, beat the yolks into the pumpkin.
- Whisk the egg whites until stiff and fold into the mixture.
- Pour into an oiled casserole dish and bake at 180°C for 30-45 mins until risen and set. Serve at once.

vegetable fritters

3/4 cup plain wholemeal flour
1/2 tsp garam masala
1 tsp salt
1/4 tsp turmeric
pinch of chilli powder

1/2 cup water
1 clove garlic, crushed
2 cups mixed vegetables, chopped
oil for frying

- Stir together the flour, garam masala, salt, turmeric and chilli. Add the water gradually and beat into a thick batter. Add the garlic, beat again, then allow to stand for 30 mins.
- Mix in the veggies.
- Heat 1cm depth oil in a large frying pan, and drop spoonfuls of the batter into the oil - allow room to spread.
- Fry for a couple of minutes each side, until golden.
- Serve with a curry or spicy plum sauce.

Beans & Lentils

Beans take a little more forethought and preparation than most foods; lentils on the other hand are pretty quick and convenient.

Chick peas, soya beans and kidney beans should be rinsed thoroughly before use, as they tend to be dusty – also hunt through for bits of grit and stone which the graders eyes have missed.

To shorten the cooking time, you can soak beans overnight in 3 cups water per cup of beans. Next day, boil the beans in fresh water. Cooking times vary according to the bean and the texture you want. Soya beans take several hours; chick peas about 1½ hrs; haricot, kidney, lima beans etc take 45 mins – 1 hr. As a general rule, simmer the beans in a covered pan, and check every 15 mins for softness, and that they haven't boiled dry.

For busy people, and those who find it difficult to remember to soak the beans the day before, beans can be frozen after cooking, and can be added to sauces straight from the freezer. To freeze – drain the cooked beans and spread out on baking trays in a single layer. Freeze, and put into plastic bags to store.

Lentils generally don't need a pre-soak as they cook quickly, but a soak for an hour or so shortens the cooking time quite a bit. Many of our recipes use brown lentils and usually they are sufficiently cooked when brought to the boil and simmered for 10-15 mins. Red lentils and split peas are usually cooked to a mush - beware them burning on the bottom of the pan as they get soupy.

GREEK CHICKPEAS

1 large eggplant, cubed
3 onions, sliced
500g tomatoes, cubed
2 cups cooked chickpeas

¼ cup olive oil
1½ cups stock
Salt & Pepper
Pinch of rosemary & basil

- Heat ½ the olive oil in a frying pan & fry the onions over a moderate heat until brown.
- Remove the onions, add the rest of the oil and fry the chunks of eggplant until just browning and soft.
- Layer a casserole with eggplant, chickpeas, onions & tomatoes.
- Season the stock well, add the herbs and pour over casserole.
- Cover with a lid and bake at 180°C for 1hr.
- Serve with rice, or with good bread & salad.

Sherwood Lentil Pie

2 cups lentils

2 onions, chopped

2 cloves garlic, crushed

3 tbs. tomato paste

1 tbs. soy sauce

mashed potato, enough for topping

mixed herbs and seasonings

Nuttelex

- Cook the lentils for 15 mins, wash and drain well.
- Sauté the onions and garlic in a little oil.
- Add the tomato paste and cook until the onion starts to brown.
- Mix in soy sauce and cooked lentils.
- Put the mixture into an ovenproof dish.
- Add herbs and seasonings to mashed potato, and enough Nuttelex to make it soft and creamy.
- Cover the lentil mixture with piped mashed potato.
- Brown in the oven or under the grill.

BRONWYN'S LENTIL PIE

A real favourite at the restaurant — particularly good for tempting sceptical meat eaters.

1 cup green lentils	25g butter
500g cooked potatoes	1 cup cream
3 zucchinis	50g grated cheddar cheese
100g mushrooms	Salt + pepper
1 clove garlic	

- Put the lentils in a pan with plenty of water, bring to the boil, + simmer for 15 mins until just tender. Drain in a collander + rinse in cold water.

- Slice the zucchinis and mushrooms thinly, and chop garlic.

- Fry the zucchinis and garlic in butter, stirring occasionally until just turning translucent, add the mushrooms + fry a further 2 mins. Remove from heat.

- To assemble — put the lentils into a casserole + cover with the zucchini + mushroom mix. Slice the potatoes thinly + arrange on top. Pour the cream over the potatoes + sprinkle with grated cheese.

- Bake at 200°C for about 20 mins until the cheese is tinged golden and the cream bubbles at the side.

Lentil Burgers

2 cups cooked brown or green lentils
1 cup cooked potatoes
1 cup brown breadcrumbs
¼ cup sesame seeds
¼ cup sunflower seeds
½ cup finely chopped almonds
1 clove crushed garlic
1 onion, finely chopped
Small bunch of fresh herbs e.g. basil, oregano, rosemary, thyme, parsley. etc.
salt & pepper
oil for frying

- Mash the potato well and mix in the lentils.
- Add the breadcrumbs, sesame & sunflower seeds, chopped almond, onion & garlic.
- Finely chop the herbs, and add to the mixture with the salt & pepper. Mix everything together well.
- Divide into portions and form into burger shapes.
- Heat about 1 cm. oil in a heavy frying pan and fry the burgers over a moderate heat about 5 mins each side.
- Pop the burgers into good wholemeal buns stuffed with salad, chutney or fresh tomato sauce.

Lentil & Zucchini Khoreshe

75g green or brown lentils
1 large onion, sliced
1 clove garlic, crushed
3 small zucchinis, sliced
2 tbs tomato paste
2 tbs olive oil

1 tsp turmeric
½ tsp cumin
½ tsp cinnamon
¼ tsp chilli
Salt & pepper

- Cover the lentils with water and simmer for 30-40 mins until tender but not mushy. Drain and set aside.
- Heat the oil in a large pan and fry the onions and garlic for 5 mins. Add the zucchinis and fry 2 mins.
- Add the spices, fry 1 min then add the tomato paste and 1½ cups water.
- Season well, add the lentils, and simmer for 15-20 mins until the zucchinis are tender.
- Serve with Iranian Pilau or on a bed of cous cous for a Middle Eastern flavour

LENTIL LOAF

500g cooked brown lentils
300g cooked brown rice
125g chopped onions
150g chopped celery

150g chopped nuts
1 tsp rubbed sage
1 tsp stock powder
salt & pepper

- The lentils for this loaf should be quite well cooked, then drained but not rinsed, so they are quite mushy.
- Saute the onions & celery in a little oil until translucent - about 5 mins.
- Combine all the ingredients and mix really well, preferably with your hands, until the mixture begins to stick together.
- Pack into well greased loaf tins and bake at 180°C for 30-45 mins, and serve with a tasty tomato or mushroom sauce.

Cheese & Walnut Loaf

1 cup chopped onions
1 cup chopped walnuts
1 cup chopped sunflower seeds
1 cup grated carrot
1 cup chopped celery
1 cup chopped capsicum
2 eggs
2 cups brown breadcrumbs
1 × 500g can crushed tomatoes, drained
2 cups grated cheddar cheese
3 cloves garlic, crushed
dash of paprika
dash of chilli powder

~ Prepare all the ingredients and put them all together in a large bowl. Mix very well.
~ Pack into well greased loaf tins
~ Bake at 180°C for about 1 hour.

NUT TERRINE

½ cup onion, finely chopped
½ cup celery, finely chopped
1 cup walnuts, chopped
1 cup peanut butter
500g. block of tofu
A handful of mixed fresh herbs

1 dsp. of mustard
1 dsp. of soya sauce
½ cup rolled oats
¼ cup sunflower seeds
¼ cup sesame seeds
salt & pepper
a little oil for frying

- Heat a little oil in a frying pan and fry the onions & celery gently for 10 mins.
- Assemble all the other ingredients and mix everything together in a big bowl.
- Pack the mixture into well greased loaf tins and cover with foil.
- Bake at 180°C for 45 mins. – 1 hr. Remove the foil for 10 mins. before the loaf is cooked to brown it.
- The terrine can be served hot, with a gravy or sauce, or cold in sandwiches, pita breads, as a starter, with a salad ......

MUSHROOM LOAF

75g. boughal (cracked wheat - soaked)
1 block tofu
½ cup vegetable oil
500g. sliced mushrooms
3 tbs. dry sherry
2 onions finely chopped
2 cloves crushed garlic
2 cups breadcrumbs
1 cup of potatoes
1 tbs. tamari
1 tbs. basil (fresh)
1 tbs. tarragon
salt and pepper

- Sauté onions and garlic in oil.
- Add mushrooms & herbs.
- Add sherry - cook to reduce liquid.
- Process tofu with a little oil.
- Mix all ingredients together.
- Bake in a moderate oven for 30-40 minutes.

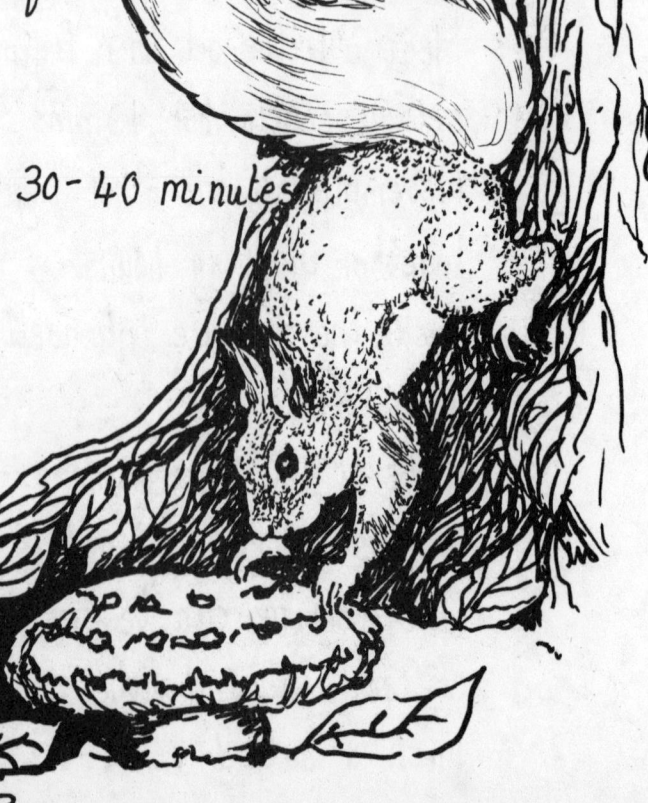

Nicks Nut Loaf

2 cups cooked brown lentils
1 cup cooked brown rice
1 cup cooked chick peas
1 cup ground cashew nuts
½ cup ground almonds
 salt & pepper
½ cup grated carrot
1 tsp tamari
2 tsp miso
2 tsp chopped fresh sage or thyme
⅓ cup good vegetable stock

- Whiz the chick peas with the stock until quite fine.
- Mix together all the ingredients until well combined, seasoning to taste with salt & pepper.
- Pack into a well oiled baking tin or loaf tin and cover with foil.
- Bake at 180°C for 30 mins, then remove the foil and bake for a further 15 mins until golden and firm.
- Serve hot with your favourite sauce.

Veggy & Almond Bake

5 cups diced veggies - carrot, cauli, zucchini, celery & co

1 cup chopped onion

2 cloves garlic, crushed

1½ cups almonds

2 cups water

5 tbs butter

3 tbs plain wholemeal flour

1 tsp horseradish

½ tsp dry mustard

1 tbs tamari

dash of Tabasco or chilli

½ cup brown breadcrumbs

salt & pepper

- Saute the onions & garlic in 2 tbs butter for 5 mins. Add the veggies and saute gently for about 15 mins until tender.
- Toast the almonds in the oven at 180°C until golden, turning often.
- Place one cup of almonds in a processor or blender, and whiz with 2 cups water until smooth & milky.
- Melt 3 tbs butter in a pan, mix in the flour, then whisk in the almond puree and heat slowly until thickened. Simmer for 10 mins, and add the horseradish, mustard, Tabasco, Tamari, and seasonings. Stir the sauce into the veggies.
- Pour the mixture into a buttered casserole, sprinkle with the breadcrumbs and remaining ½ cup chopped almonds.
- Bake at 200°C for 15 mins.

Sweet Potato & Leek Loaf

2 tbs oil
1 cup cooked soya beans
1 bunch leeks, sliced
3 cloves garlic, crushed
5 medium sweet potatoes
½ cup milk or soy milk
½ tsp salt
1 tsp ground coriander
1 tsp nutmeg
¼ tsp chilli

Topping
1 cup wheatgerm
1 cup wholemeal flour
½ tsp coriander
½ tsp cumin
¾ cup butter (or Nuttelex)
Pinch of salt

* Saute the leeks and garlic in oil until soft. Steam or boil the sweet potatoes until tender, then mash with the milk.
* Mix all the loaf ingredients together and spoon into an oiled casserole dish.
* For the topping, mix together all the dry ingredients and rub in the butter until the mixture is crumbly. Sprinkle topping over the sweet potato and leek loaf.
* Bake at 180°C for about 40 mins until the top is golden brown.

OUR ASIAN RICE

225g cooked brown rice
3 tbs oil
12 shallots, chopped
1 clove garlic, crushed
4 sticks celery, diced
150g can sliced waterchestnuts
1 lb beanshoots
a handful chopped parsley

1 tsp oregano
½ tsp basil
100g sunflower seed kernals
2 tbs fresh ginger, grated
175g honey
100 mls tamari
1 tbs lemon juice

▽ Heat the oil in a wok and fry the shallots and garlic & ginger a minute or two. Add the celery and fry for another minute.

▽ Toss in the water chestnuts, beanshoots & parsley and fry for yet another minute, stirring often.

▽ Add the herbs & sunflower seeds.

▽ Combine the honey, tamari & lemon juice and stir into the veggies, and add the cooked rice. Mix well and season with extra salt & pepper if you feel it needs any more.

▽ Note – to cook the rice, boil in plenty of salted water for 30 mins (approx), then drain & rinse in cold water.

FALAFEL

1 medium potato, cooked & mashed
1 bunch parsley or coriander
2 small onions
3 cups cooked chick peas
3 tbs. oil
¼ cup sesame seed meal or tahini

2 cloves garlic, crushed
juice of 1 lemon
pinch of cayenne
pinch of paprika
salt & pepper

- Grind the chick peas in a processor or through a mincer.
- Finely chop the onion and fry in the oil for 5 mins.
- Remove from the heat and mix together with all the other ingredients.
- Form into small balls, using about 2 tbs mixture.
- Place on an oiled baking tray and bake for about 20 mins at 180°C, turning them over after 10 mins to brown the underside. They are also yummy deep fried.

Swedish Casserole

1 bunch leeks, sliced
200g mushrooms
2 large carrots, sliced
2 large parsnips, sliced
50g butter

25g flour
500mls milk
½ cup dry white wine
2 tbs horseradish sauce
Salt & pepper
1 tsp chopped dill

Croustade topping ~
50g brown breadcrumbs
50g ground nuts
50g melted butter
1 clove garlic, crushed

♡ Melt the butter in a pan, add the leeks and saute gently for 3 mins. Add the sliced mushrooms and fry briskly for 3 mins. Toss in the flour, stirring rapidly and mix in the white wine. Gradually add the milk and heat until thickened and a smooth sauce is acheived. Season with salt, pepper, horseradish and dill and set aside.

♡ Steam the sliced carrots and parsnips for 10 mins until just tender, then add them to the sauce. Pour the mixture into a casserole dish.

♡ To make the croustade topping, mix the melted butter with the breadcrumbs, nuts and garlic, add a little pepper and sprinkle over the top of the casserole.

♡ Bake at 180°C for 20-30 mins until the casserole is bubbling and browning on top.

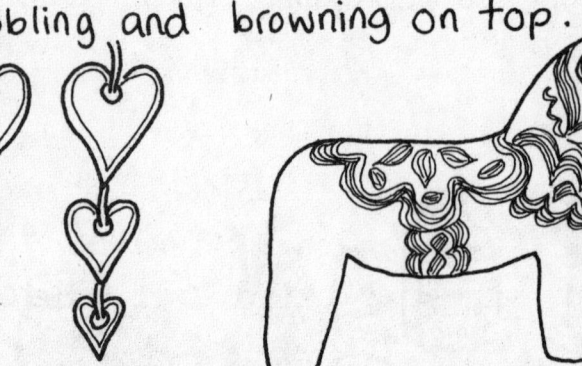

CHILLI BEANS with CORN CHIPS

2 cups cooked red kidney beans
1 large onion
2 cloves garlic, crushed
small piece fresh ginger
2 carrots
1 capsicum
3 tbs oil
2 tbs plain wholemeal flour
135 ml can tomato paste
1 tsp chilli powder
½ tsp cumin powder
small bunch fresh basil
½ litre stock or water
salt & pepper
1 packet corn chips
50g grated Cheddar cheese

- Dice the onion, carrot and capsicum into 1cm dice
- Heat the oil in a saucepan and add the onion, garlic and grated ginger for 3 mins; toss in the carrots & capsicum and fry for 5 mins.
- Add the chilli & cumin, fry 1 min, then add the flour and tomato paste and gradually stir in the stock or water.
- Chop the basil and add to the sauce, season well and simmer for 15 mins, stirring frequently.
- Remove from the heat, add the beans, and if there's time, allow to stand for ½ hr.
- Pour into a shallow casserole, sprinkle with corn chips and cheese, and bake at 200°C for 20-30 mins.
- Serve with jacket potatoes, sour cream and sweetcorn.

BEAN GOULASH

250g red kidney beans
2 small onions, diced
2 zucchinis, sliced
1 large green capsicum, diced
2 tbs oil
1 small can sweetcorn
3 tbs tomato paste
1 tbs paprika
Salt & pepper

- Soak the beans overnight in plenty of water; next day simmer them for 40-60 mins until tender. Drain the beans.
- Meanwhile heat the oil in a large pot and fry the onions gently for 5 mins. Add the capsicum, fry for 3 mins then and the zucchini and fry a further 3 mins.
- Toss in the paprika and saute quickly, then add the tomato paste and sweetcorn and enough water to make a thick sauce. Cook gently for 10 mins.
- Add the drained beans, season well and cook or let stand for 5 mins for the flavours to blend.
- Serve with rice or noodles, a dollop of sour cream and a sprinkle of dill or paprika.

HONEYED PUMPKIN

- 1kg pumpkin
- ½ cup gluten flour
- 1 cup water
- ½ onion
- 1 tbs tamari
- 8 shallots, chopped
- 2 tbs honey
- 2 tbs tamari
- 1 clove garlic, crushed
- 1 knob ginger, grated

◀ Put the gluten flour in a bowl & add 1 cup water, do not mix, just leave for at least an hour to absorb the water.

◀ Turn out of the bowl & cut into small cubes.

◀ Put the onion & 1 tbs tamari in a pan with lots of water, bring to boil and add the gluten cubes; poach for 5 mins. Drain and set aside.

◀ Meanwhile, peel & chop the pumpkin into small cubes.

◀ Heat the oil and stir fry the pumpkin for 5 mins, then add the shallots, garlic & ginger, honey & tamari and the gluten. Cover with a lid and stew gently until the pumpkin is tender - 10-15 mins.

◀ Serve as a side dish with other Chinese style dishes such as sweet & sour veggies & rice.

Lemongrass and Tofu Curry

1 onion, sliced
2 potatoes, sliced
3 cloves garlic
1 chilli pod, chopped
½ tsp coriander
½ tsp turmeric

1 tsp cumin
2 tbs oil or ghee
6 cups lemongrass tea
2 cups shredded spinach
1 cup carrots in matchsticks

1 tray tofu, cut in triangles and drained
Oil for deep frying
Salt & pepper

- Saute the onion in the oil for 5 mins. Add the garlic and spices and saute gently for a further 5 mins.
- Add the potatoes and lemon grass tea and simmer for about 1 hr.
- Add the spinach and carrots, salt and pepper and simmer for a further 5 mins.
- To prepare the tofu, pat the tofu triangles dry, heat the oil and fry the triangles until golden. Drain well and keep warm.
- Serve the curry with cooked rice and raita (p.191) and garnish with the tofu triangles on top.

Chick Pea Curry

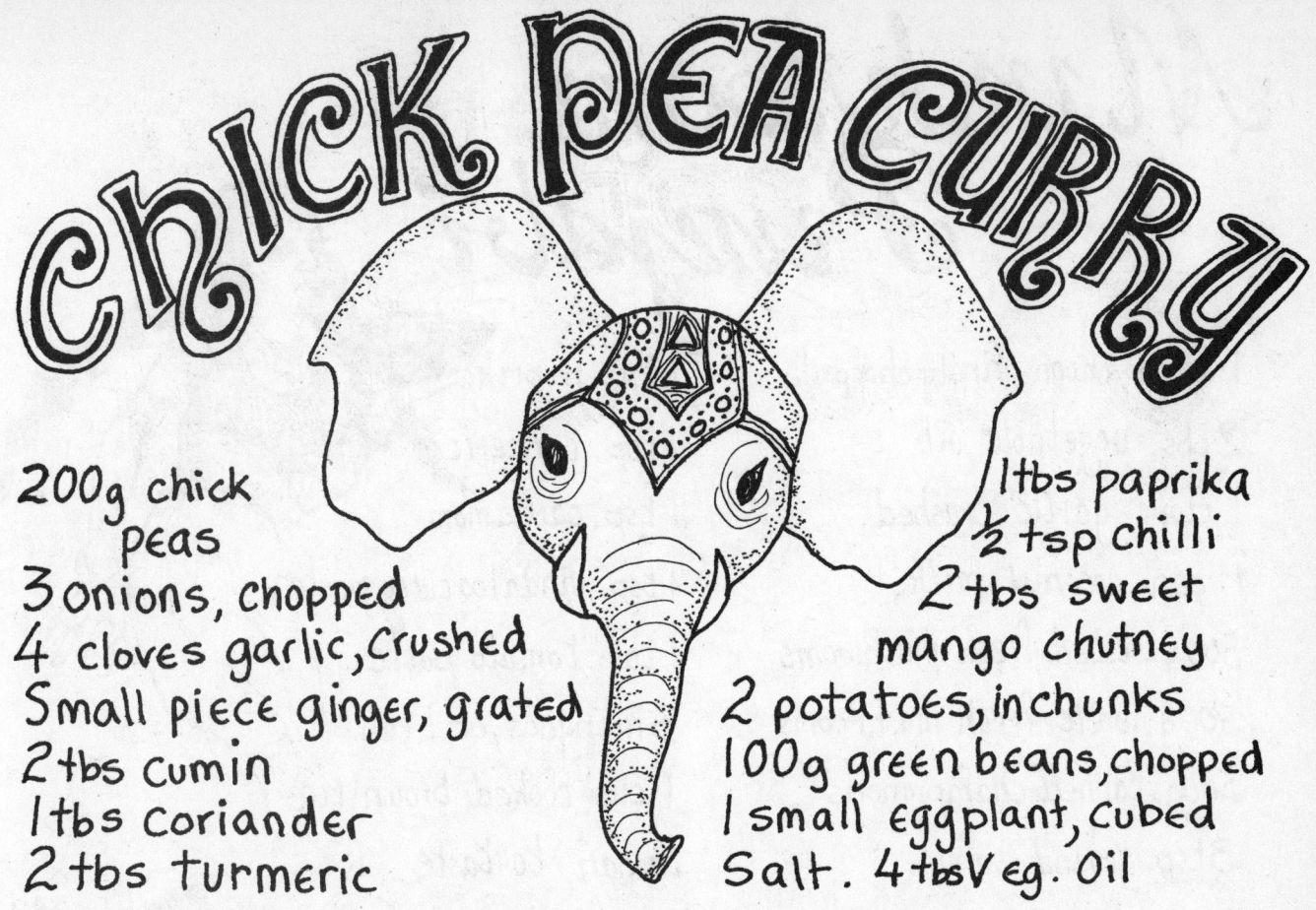

- 200g chick peas
- 3 onions, chopped
- 4 cloves garlic, crushed
- Small piece ginger, grated
- 2 tbs cumin
- 1 tbs coriander
- 2 tbs turmeric
- 1 tbs paprika
- ½ tsp chilli
- 2 tbs sweet mango chutney
- 2 potatoes, in chunks
- 100g green beans, chopped
- 1 small eggplant, cubed
- Salt. 4 tbs Veg. Oil

⊙ Soak the peas overnight in plenty of water. Next day, boil for an hour or so until very tender.

⊙ Meanwhile, heat the oil in a pan and fry the onions, garlic & ginger gently for 10 mins. Add the spices and fry 2 mins, then add 2 cups water.

⊙ Add the vegetables, season well with salt and simmer for ½ hr until tender.

⊙ Add the chick peas and chutney and cook gently for 10 mins.

⊙ Serve the curry with rice and traditional accompaniments ~ yoghurt, papadams, chutneys, coconut & bananas.

Mushroom Punjabi

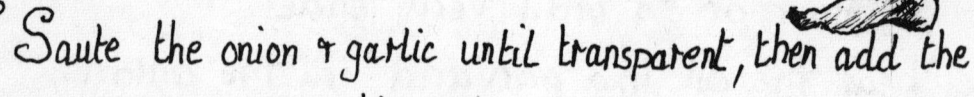

1 large onion, finely chopped
2 tbs. vegetable oil
1 clove garlic, crushed
1 can coconut milk
500g. sliced fresh mushrooms
500g. whole fresh mushrooms
500g. canned champignons
3 tsp. ground cumin
1 tsp. ground coriander
1 tsp. paprika
1 tsp. turmeric
1 tsp. cardamom
1 tsp. vindaloo curry paste
1 tbs. tomato paste
3 mangoes, or 1 can
1 cup cooked brown rice
tamari to taste

- Saute the onion & garlic until transparent, then add the curry spices and stir well.
- Add the sliced mushrooms & coconut milk and cook gently for 5 mins.
- Add the drained champignons, tomato paste, and simmer for 5 mins.
- Finally stir in the whole mushrooms, sliced mangoes and tamari to taste.
- Put the rice in the bottom of an ovenproof dish and pour over the mushroom sauce.
- Bake at 180°c. for 15 mins., and serve with green salad and papadams.

DHAL

1 cup red lentils
1 tsp. cumin
1 tsp. poppy seeds
½ tsp. cinnamon
½ tsp. cardamon
1 tsp. turmeric

1 tsp. paprika
4 cloves
2 onions, chopped
2 cloves garlic, crushed
1 cup coconut
2 tbs oil
salt & pepper

- Cover the lentils with water & cook until mushy.
- Grind together all the spices.
- Heat the oil and fry the onions & garlic until turning golden.
- Add the spices and fry for 2 mins., then add the coconut, fry 1 min.
- Finally add the cooked lentils and mix well. Remove from the heat and allow to stand for at least ½ hr. to allow flavours to blend, then reheat and serve with rice and a vegetable curry.

Eggplant & Potato Curry

- 1 tbs dark mustard seeds
- 1 tbs light mustard seeds
- 3 tbs oil
- 2 medium onions, chopped
- 3 cloves garlic, crushed
- 1 small piece ginger, grated
- 2 medium eggplants, chopped
- 500g washed potatoes, sliced thinly
- 1 can coconut milk
- 1 tbs green masala paste
- 1 tbs turmeric
- ½ tbs cumin powder
- 2 tbs fresh coriander leaves
- Salt & pepper.

- Heat the oil in a large pan and throw in the mustard seeds ~ fry for a couple of minutes without burning them.
- Add the garlic, ginger & onions and fry over a medium heat until the onions are browning & translucent.
- Add the masala paste, cumin & turmeric, fry for 2 mins, then pour in the coconut milk and add the sliced potatoes.
- Cook gently for about 15 mins, stirring often, and adding a little stock or water if the sauce begins to catch on the base of the pan. Add the eggplant, and cook gently for a further 15-20 mins until the vegetables are tender.
- Finally, add the chopped fresh coriander leaves and season to taste.
- Serve with brown rice, Indian salad, yoghurt, chutney & pappadams.

Cath's Curry Casserole

250g spinach or silverbeet
2 carrots, sliced
1 large zucchini, sliced
1 large onion, sliced
200g cauliflower florets
200g cabbage, shredded

25g butter or margarine
25g plain wholewheat flour
150ml skim or whole milk
175g Edam or Cheddar cheese
2 tsp curry powder
25g fresh brown breadcrumbs

- Remove the stalks from the spinach and steam the leaves for 5 mins. Drain and cool.
- Place the other veggies in a pan and just cover with water. Boil for 10 mins, then drain and cool but keep 150mls of the cooking liquid.
- Melt the butter in a pan, stir in the flour and cook gently for 1 min. Gradually add the reserved cooking liquid and milk.
- Bring to the boil and simmer for 2 mins, stirring all the time.
- Add 100g cheese, curry powder, salt & pepper.
- Place the spinach in a casserole dish, cover with the cooked veggies and pour over the sauce. Mix the remaining cheese and breadcrumbs and sprinkle over casserole.
- Bake at 190°C for 30 mins until browned & bubbling.

TOFU & VEGGIE CURRY

1 tray tofu
2 onions, finely chopped
3 cloves garlic, crushed
small piece of ginger, grated
1 tsp each of paprika, turmeric, cumin & coriander
1 tsp vindaloo curry paste
4 cups mixed veggies, eg carrots, capsicum, broccoli etc
oil for frying
wholemeal flour
salt & pepper

- Cut the tofu into chunky cubes and toss them in flour.
- Heat 1cm depth oil in a pan and fry the tofu until golden on all sides. Drain the tofu well and set aside.
- Use some of remaining oil to fry the onions, garlic and ginger gently for 5 mins.
- Add the spices and curry paste and fry 1min then add 2 tbs flour and enough stock or water to form a smooth sauce. Season well and simmer for 10 mins.
- Steam or stir fry the veggies until just tender, then add to the sauce along with the tofu. Heat thoroughly.
- Serve the curry over brown rice.

IRANIAN PILAU

400g long grain brown rice
2 small onions, sliced
1 clove garlic, crushed
1 large carrot, diced
100g fresh or frozen peas
1 green capsicum, diced
4 tbs olive oil

50g dried apricots
50g raisins
50g almonds, chopped
2 tsp grated orange peel
½ tsp nutmeg
1 tsp cinnamon
Salt & pepper

- Soak the apricots and raisins overnight in a cup of water.
- Cook the rice in plenty of water until just tender. Drain and rinse in cold water.
- Heat 3 tbs oil in a large frying pan or wok and fry the onions and garlic for 5 mins. Add the carrot and capsicum and stir fry for a further 5 mins. Add the peas and almonds, cook for 3 mins then remove from the heat.
- Drain the liquid from the fruit, slice the apricots and fry the fruit in the remaining 1 tbs oil with the cinnamon and nutmeg for 3 mins.
- Mix together the rice, fruit, veggies and peel, season well and turn into a casserole dish. Heat through in a covered dish for 20 mins at 180°C.
- Serve hot with lentil & zucchini khoreshe.

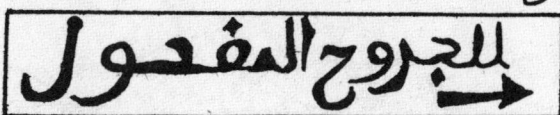

BALTHAZAARS BAZAAR →

Lebanese Pilav

2 cups cooked brown rice
1 cup cooked green lentils
2 tbs sesame seeds
2 onions, sliced
2 cloves garlic, crushed
3 tbs olive oil
2 tsp basil
1 tsp oregano
½ bunch silverbeet
3 tomatoes, chopped
Salt & pepper

✦ Wash, remove stems and shred the silverbeet.
✦ Heat the oil in a large frying pan and saute the onions until browning, stirring often.
✦ Add the garlic and sesame seeds, fry for 2 mins, then add the herbs and tomatoes and fry over a high heat for 3 mins.
✦ Add the chopped silverbeet, cook until just wilted, then add the lentils and brown rice.
✦ Season well with salt & pepper and cook for 5 mins until quite dry.
✦ Serve with salad, or a bean or vegetable stew.

COUS COUS CASABLANCA

2 onions, sliced
2 cloves garlic, crushed
2 carrots, sliced
1 parsnip, sliced
1 eggplant, cubed
1 medium potato, cubed
A handful green beans, halved
3 ripe tomatoes, chopped
3 tbs oil

1 cup sultanas
1 cup cooked chick peas
2 tbs turmeric
½ tbs chilli
1 tbs cumin
1 tbs coriander
Salt & pepper
½ pkt (250g) cous cous

O Heat the the oil in a large pot, and fry the onions for 5 mins until begining to brown. Add the garlic & spices, fry gently for 2 mins, then add the prepared vegetables, fry for 1 min, then add enough water or stock to barely cover the veggies.
O Add the cooked chick peas, sultanas, salt & pepper and simmer for 20-30 mins until the veggies are tender.
O To prepare the cous cous, put it in a bowl and cover with 2cm depth of water. Leave for 20 mins for the cous cous to absorb the water.
O To heat and flavour the cous cous, place it in a fine sieve and steam over the vegetables for 10-15 mins with a lid on top.
O Serve the cous cous on a plate with the sauce over the top.

TOFU

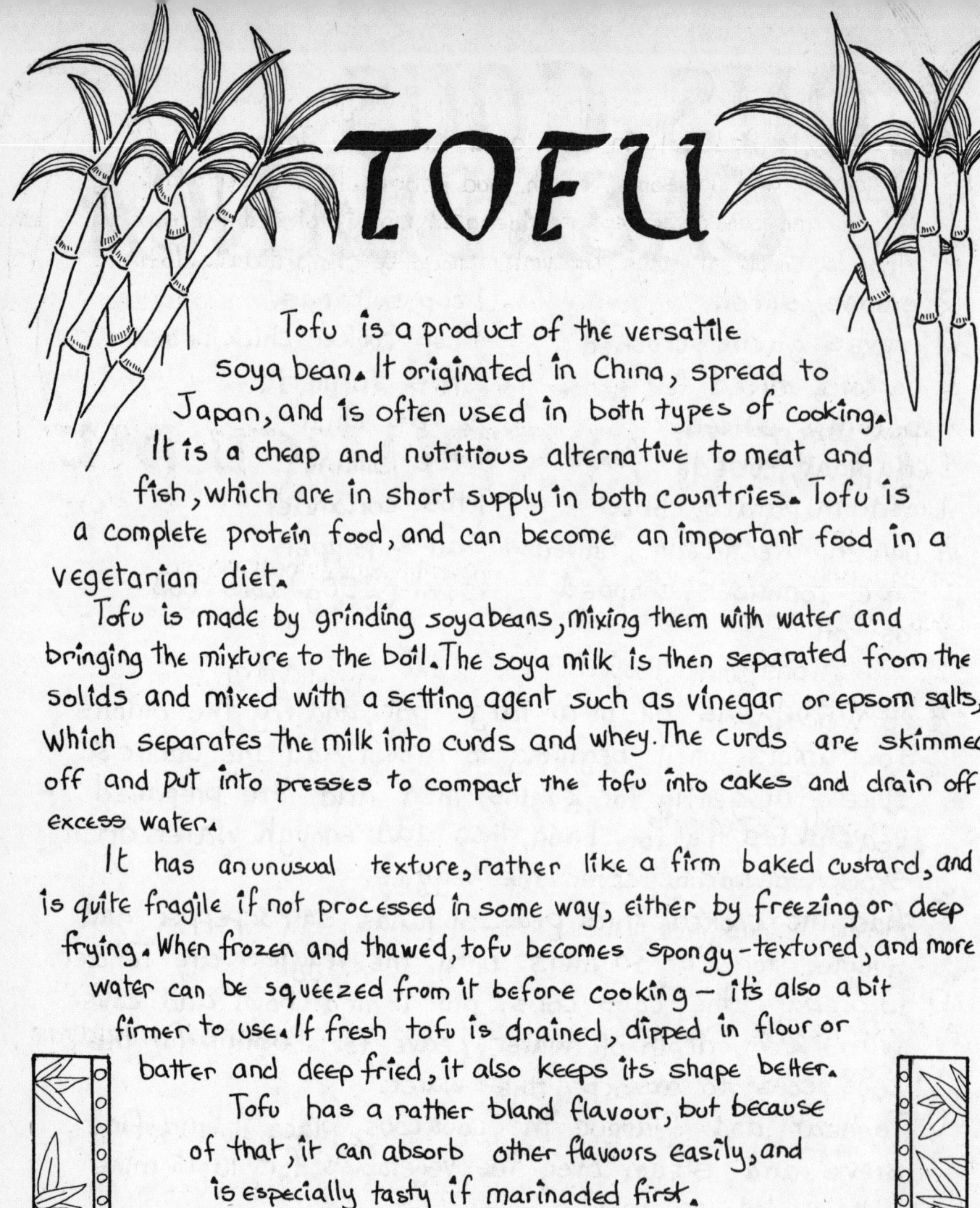

Tofu is a product of the versatile soya bean. It originated in China, spread to Japan, and is often used in both types of cooking. It is a cheap and nutritious alternative to meat and fish, which are in short supply in both countries. Tofu is a complete protein food, and can become an important food in a vegetarian diet.

Tofu is made by grinding soya beans, mixing them with water and bringing the mixture to the boil. The soya milk is then separated from the solids and mixed with a setting agent such as vinegar or epsom salts, which separates the milk into curds and whey. The curds are skimmed off and put into presses to compact the tofu into cakes and drain off excess water.

It has an unusual texture, rather like a firm baked custard, and is quite fragile if not processed in some way, either by freezing or deep frying. When frozen and thawed, tofu becomes spongy-textured, and more water can be squeezed from it before cooking — it's also a bit firmer to use. If fresh tofu is drained, dipped in flour or batter and deep fried, it also keeps its shape better.

Tofu has a rather bland flavour, but because of that, it can absorb other flavours easily, and is especially tasty if marinaded first.

It is not widely availible yet, but you should be able to find tofu in any good Chinese or Japanese grocer, and in some health food stores. It is a perishable food and should be kept refrigerated, and if stored for more than a couple of days, the water should be changed daily. Tofu can be frozen, but this does change the texture quite dramatically.

Here are a few recipes for you to try.......

TOFU & SPINACH PIE

500g	tofu	1 quantity wholewheat pastry
1 bunch	spinach or silver beet	or
2	onions, finely chopped	½ pkt filo pastry
½ cup	wheatgerm	or
¼ tsp	nutmeg	½ pkt kataifi pastry
	salt & pepper	
½ tsp	your favourite herbs	

- Fry the onions in a little oil until golden.
- Steam the spinach for 5 mins until wilted, drain and chop.
- Crumble the tofu, and mix with the onions, spinach, wheatgerm and seasonings.
- The filling is now ready to use in a wholewheat pastry pie, filo rolls, or rolled in kataifi pastry and baked on a tomato sauce.

Vegan Note — to make this dish vegan, use oil or non-milk margarine in the pastry or to brush the filo or kataifi pastry.

TOFU & SPINACH LOAF

- 3 tbs vegetable oil
- 1 large onion
- 150g mushrooms
- 1 cup walnuts
- 1 bunch silverbeet or spinach
- 1½ trays tofu
- ½ cup wheat germ
- 1 tbs dry sherry
- 2 tbs worcester sauce
- pinch of nutmeg
- 1 tbs tamari
- salt & pepper

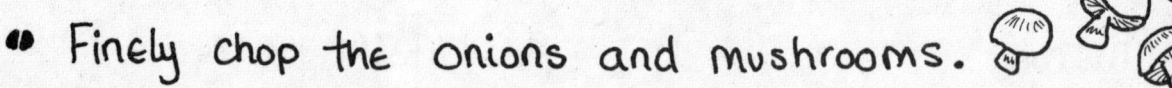

- Finely chop the onions and mushrooms.
- Heat the oil in a large pan or wok and fry the onions & mushrooms for 5 mins.
- Grind the nuts until mealy, and finely chop the spinach. Add these two to the onions + mushrooms. along with the sherry & worcester sauce. Cook for 5 mins.
- Remove from the heat and crumble in the tofu, add the wheat germ & nutmeg and season with tamari, salt & pepper.
- Bake in an oiled casserole at 180°C for 30 mins.
- Serve with a mushroom sauce - either creamy or gravy type sauce.

TOFU SATAYS
with Peanut Sauce

½ pineapple
2 apples
2 capsicums, 1 red & 1 green
500g tofu, cubed
2 tbs tamari
1 tsp coriander
1 tsp cumin
1 tsp turmeric
Pinch chilli powder

Peanut Sauce:-
1 cup crunchy peanut butter
½ tsp chilli powder
1 onion, chopped
1 clove garlic, crushed
1 cup coconut milk
2 tbs tamari
1 tbs raw sugar
2 tbs lemon juice
2 tbs oil

- Marinade the tofu in tamari, coriander, cumin, turmeric and chilli for a few hours.
- Cut the pineapple, apple & capsicum into chunky pieces, and thread the tofu and veggies onto wooden satay sticks. Brush with a little oil.
- Grill or bake the satays in a hot oven for 10 mins.
- To make the sauce — heat the oil and fry the onions & garlic for 5 mins. Add the peanut butter and mix in the coconut milk, tamari, sugar, chilli and lemon juice. Add a little water if the sauce is too thick. Simmer 10 mins.
- Serve the satays on a bed of fried rice with sauce over.

TOFU CHINESE STLE

1 tray tofu
2 eggplants
2 onions, sliced
1 clove garlic, crushed
small piece of fresh ginger
1 oz dried Chinese mushrooms

2-3 tbs tamari
2 tbs malt vinegar
½ tsp aniseed
¼ cup dry sherry
2 tbs corn flour
vegetable oil

- Cut the eggplant into long thin strips, about 1cm wide, sprinkle them with salt, leave for ½ hr, then rinse & drain.
- Cover the dried mushrooms with boiling water & leave for 20 mins. Slice the mushies & keep the water.
- Heat some oil in a wok and fry the eggplant until browned and tender, set them aside.
- Fry the onions, garlic & grated ginger for 5 mins, keep stirring, then add the sliced mushrooms.
- Mix together the tamari, vinegar, aniseed, sherry, mushroom water and cornflour, and add to onions. Cook until the sauce thickens, then add the eggplant and tofu, cut in chunks.
- Serve with steamed brown rice.

TOFU À LA KING

300g. tofu, in chunky cubes
2 onions
1 clove garlic, crushed
1 capsicum (large)
250 g. mushrooms
¼ cup dry sherry

1 tsp. basil
250 mls white sauce (p.190)
¼ cup soya cream
50 g. Nuttelex
salt and pepper

- Chop the onions and garlic and fry gently in Nuttelex.
- Chop or slice capsicums, and add to the onions, slice the mushrooms and add with the basil. Fry for a few minutes.
- Add the sherry and boil briskly to evaporate half of the liquid.
- Reduce the heat, season well and add the white sauce and tofu, and heat gently until thoroughly warmed. Just before serving, add the soya cream.
- Serve tofu à la King over rice or pasta, or in filo rolls.

Battered Tofu in Sweet & Sour Sauce

1 tray tofu, cut in cubes
4 tbs tamari
2 tsp sugar
1 tsp grated fresh ginger
1 small can ginger pickle
3 tbs oil
1 large onion
1 bunch spring onions
¼ cauliflower, in florettes

1 red capsicum
100g mushrooms
1 stick celery
1 pineapple
2 tbs tomato paste
½ cup wholemeal flour
1 tbs soya compound
water
1 tbs vinegar
2 tbs cornflour

- Combine the tamari, ginger, and pickle liquid and marinade the tofu in this for at least an hour.
- Make a thick batter from the flour and soya compound and water. Drain the tofu chunks, dip in the batter and deep fry until golden brown.
- Slice all the veggies thinly and stir-fry in a wok for about 10 mins. Add the pineapple.
- Mix the tomato paste, vinegar, cornflour, marinade and a cup of water and add to the wok. Stir until the sauce thickens, and add the tofu chunks.
- Serve the sweet & sour battered tofu with plenty of brown rice.

TOFU TERIYAKI & FRIED RICE

Tofu Marinade:-
- 400g tofu, sliced
- 1 cup apple juice
- 1 clove garlic, finely chopped
- A piece ginger, finely chopped
- 4 tbs tamari
- 1 tbs malt vinegar
- 1 tbs raw sugar

Fried Rice:-
- 2 onions, sliced
- 1 clove garlic, finely chopped
- 1 carrots, diced
- 2 sticks celery, diced
- 1 capsicum, diced
- 50g beans, sliced
- 50g peas
- 200g brown rice
- ½ tsp turmeric
- ½ tsp paprika
- ¼ tsp chilli powder
- salt & pepper
- 2 tbs oil

- Mix all the ingredients for the marinade and pour over the tofu. Leave to mellow for a few hours.
- Meanwhile, prepare the fried rice. Put the rice in a pan with plenty of water and boil for 15-20 mins until just tender.
- Drain and rinse in cold water.
- Heat the oil and fry all the veggies together, stirring often, until just turning brown and tender.
- Add the seasonings and rice.
- To serve:- put the tofu and marinade in a shallow ovenproof dish and bake at 200°C for 20 mins. When tofu is ready, heat the rice through, place on a serving dish and spoon the tofu and marinade over the top.

TOFU CHOW MEIN

- 1 tray tofu, cubed
- 1 cup flour
- ½ head broccoli
- 1 carrot
- 1 zucchini
- 1 capsicum
- 1 large onion
- ¼ cauliflower
- 50g mushrooms
- 2 cloves garlic
- 1 can water chestnuts
- 1 can bamboo shoots
- 2 tbs oil
- 2 tbs tomato paste
- 1 tbs cornflour
- 1 cup water
- 3 tbs tamari
- ½ tbs Chinese Five Spice
- 50g fresh egg noodles
- Oil for deep frying

- Drain the tofu well for an hour, then toss in flour and deep fry in hot oil until golden.
- Drain on kitchen paper.
- Slice the vegetables thinly and heat the oil in a wok. Add the vegetables and stir fry for 10 mins until the veggies are tender.
- Meanwhile, prepare the sauce — mix together the tomato paste, cornflour, water, tamari, five spice and juice from the water chestnuts & bamboo shoots until smooth.
- Mix the sauce into the veggies, add water-chestnuts & bamboo shoots and heat until the sauce thickens. Add the tofu chunks & heat through.
- Finally, deep fry the noodles for a few seconds until crispy.
- Serve the chow mein over a bed of rice with the crispy noodles on top.

TOFU NUGGETS in Chick Pea Batter

The Marinade ~
- ¼ cup sherry, sake or mirrin
- 1 tbs sugar
- ¼ cup tamari
- 1 tbs fresh grated ginger
- ½ cup water
- ¼ cup sesame oil

The Batter ~
- 3 tbs (heaped) chick pea flour
- 1 tbs (heaped) dried soya milk powder
- 2 cups water

Plus ~
- 1 tray tofu (500g)

- Cut the tofu into 2cm cubes.
- Mix together all the ingredients for the marinade, bring to the boil and simmer for 5 mins.
- Whilst still hot, pour the marinade over the tofu chunks and leave for 2 hrs in a refrigerator.
- Strain off the marinade and reserve as a dipping sauce and drain the tofu very well.
- Mix together the ingredients for the batter and beat until smooth.
- Dip the tofu chunks into the batter and drop into hot oil to deep fry until golden and crispy. Drain well.
- Serve the nuggets as an entree with marinade to dip into, or with rice and a curry, tomato or spicy sauce.

CURRIED TOFU LOAF

1 large onion, finely chopped
2 cloves garlic, crushed
1 small knob ginger, grated
1 bunch silverbeet
1 tray tofu, drained
1 cup rolled oats
2 tbs vegetable oil
½ block creamed coconut
1 tbs cumin seeds
1 tbs turmeric
¼ tsp chilli
Salt & pepper
Dash of Tamari

- Wash & drain the silverbeet, remove stalks and chop the leaves roughly.
- Heat the oil in a large frying pan or wok. Sauté the onions, garlic & ginger for 5 mins.
- Add the cumin seeds & turmeric & chilli, fry 2 mins, add the silver beet. Cut the creamed coconut into small pieces, add to pan and fry for 5 mins.
- Remove the pan from the heat, add the rolled oats and crumble in the tofu. Season with tamari, salt & pepper and mix well.
- Press into an oiled baking dish and bake at 200°C for about ½ hr.
- Serve with your favourite sauce.

TEMPEH

by Julie & Michael Joyce

Tempeh originated hundreds, perhaps thousands of years ago in central and East Java, but there are no known records of its origins.

Tempeh is the reason why Java, the most populated area of land on our planet, does not have a hunger problem, tempeh being their mainstay. Little did we know in early 1982, when we first ate tempeh made by Cyril & Ellie Caine of Eumundi, Sunshine Coast, that we were soon to become tempeh makers like 41,000 neighbouring families in Java.

During the previous 18 months we had come to understand the nutritional & economic value of soya beans. For this reason we made soya milk & tofu each week which supplied us with everything from cream, dips, mayonnaise, cheese & cakes; and from the okara (bean pulp), soyage rolls & loaves, biscuits & granola.

I can still remember slicing fresh tempeh, the delightful mushroomy aroma, and the delicious taste of our first tempeh chips. We soon began ordering our weekly supplies of tempeh which was then only available at Eumundi Markets, or ordered through a friend. After reading about tempeh, we realized that it is the most nutritional way to eat the whole soya bean. The growth of the rhizopus culture completely combines the cooked soya beans into a firm white cake, forming tenderizing enzymes which reduces the protein to simple amino acids which makes the soya bean easily digestible, also producing unusually high amounts of vitamin B12, making tempeh the best known source of B12 in the vegetable kingdom.

Tempeh soon became the protein mainstay in our diet, and when hearing that Cyril & Ellie were returning to the States, we were concerned that tempeh would no longer be availible. We then heard that they were looking for someone who was interested enough to spend the time required in learning the art of Tempeh making. Even now, after 12 months of tempeh making, we are still fascinated by the miraculous works of nature which occurs during the incubation for our benefit.

We enjoy making tempeh and never tire of its delicious taste and texture, and its versatility.

Julie & Michael supply Squirrels with the Tempeh they make.

Tempeh Sweet & Sour

½ packet tempeh
3 tbs tamari
1 tbs dry sherry
4 tbs oil
1 onion, sliced
4 shallots, chopped
1 capsicum, diced
8 mushrooms, sliced

1 zucchini, sliced
2 sticks celery, sliced
1 pineapple, peeled & sliced
2 tbs tomato paste
¼ cup brown vinegar
2 tbs raw sugar
1 cup water
2 tbs cornflour

- Cut the tempeh into small cubes or thin slices. Mix the tamari and sherry and pour over the tempeh. Leave to marinade for an hour or so. Drain & keep marinade, and fry the tempeh in oil until golden. Drain and set aside.
- Fry the onions & shallots in the remaining oil for 2 mins, then add the celery, capsicum, zucchini & mushrooms. Stir fry for 10 mins until tender. Add the pineapple.
- Mix together the tomato paste, vinegar, sugar, water, cornflour and marinade. Pour over the veggies, add the fried tempeh and heat until the sauce thickens.
- Serve the tempeh sweet & sour with rice or noodles.

TEMPEH KEBABS

For 6 people (12 skewers) ~
1 packet Tempeh
3 tomatoes, quatered
12 medium mushrooms
1 large onion, cut in 6
3 slices pineapple, quartered
2 zucchinis, in 6 pieces each
2 capsicums, in 6 pieces each
1 eggplant, cut into 12 chunks
3 tbs tamari
1 clove garlic, crushed
1 small piece ginger, grated
3 tbs water
Oil to brush & fry

→ Prepare all the vegetables.
→ Cut the tempeh into 24 pieces ~ slice thru width ways, then 3 x 4.
→ Mix together the tamari, garlic, ginger & water, pour over tempeh and leave for ½ hr. Drain the marinade and save to use in barbecue sauce.
→ Heat 4 tbs oil in a pan or wok and gently fry the tempeh until brown. Drain and cool.
→ Next thread the vegetables on to skewers ~ each one should have 2 pieces of tempeh and one of everything else.
→ Brush with oil and grill or bake at 200°C for 10-15 mins until sizzling.
→ Serve on a bed of rice with lots of barbecue sauce. (p55)

Tempeh Burgundy

1 pkt tempeh
2 tbs tamari
2 tbs Worcester sauce
2 tbs water
2 tbs ketjap bentang
1 large onion, chopped
1 capsicum, chopped
1 clove garlic, crushed
1 tbs cornflour

1 carrot, sliced
2 sticks celery, sliced
1 zucchini, sliced
1 small head broccoli
¼ head cauliflower
1 tsp mixed spice
1 cup red burgundy wine
2 tbs tomato paste
2 bay leaves

- Cut the tempeh into cubes. Mix together the tamari, Worcester sauce, ketjap bentang and water and soak the tempeh for an hour or more.
- Heat 3 tbs oil in a frying pan and saute the tempeh for 10 mins until richly brown. Drain well.
- Heat 2 tbs oil in a pan and fry the onion, capsicum and garlic together for 5 mins. Add the wine, tomato paste, 1 cup water, bay leaf, spice and cut vegetables and simmer for 20 mins until the veggies are tender.
- Mix the cornflour with ½ cup water and stir into the stew until the sauce has thickened.
- Add the tempeh cubes and heat through for 5 mins. Serve the stew with rice or potatoes.

HOW TO USE FILO PASTRY

When using filo, have ready a pot of melted unsalted butter & a paint brush. Work quickly or the filo will dry out.

TRIANGLES

1. Butter ½ sheet, fold in half

2. Butter again, fold in thirds

3. Place filling in one corner, butter the other end.

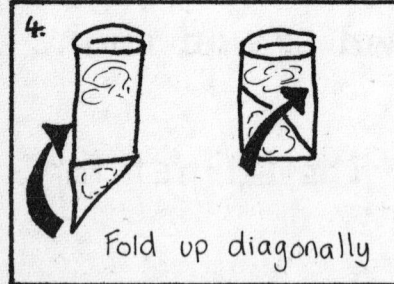
4. Fold up diagonally

5. Brush the triangles with butter & place on an oiled tray

6. Bake at 200°C for 15-20 mins until golden

STRUDELS

1. Divide stack of filo into 2 piles. Butter one sheet.

2. Place another sheet on top.

3. Place filling in one corner.

4. Roll up, tucking in the loose ends as you go.

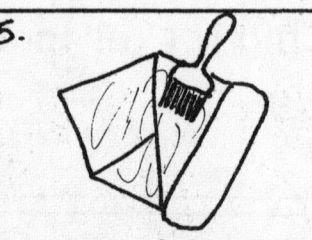
5. Put a dab of butter on the last corner to seal.

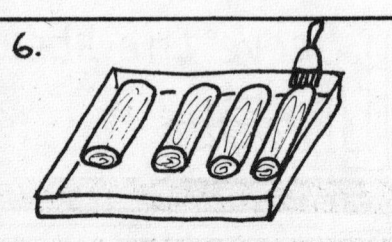
6. Brush strudels with melted butter & place on an oiled tray.

Pumpkin and Cream Cheese

1kg pumpkin
500g cream cheese
3 leeks
2 tbs butter
1 egg
50g cheddar cheese
Pinch of thyme
Salt & pepper

- Peel and trim the pumpkin and chop into 2cm cubes. Steam for 20 mins until tender but not mushy. Whilst still hot, mix into the cream cheese.
- Thinly slice the leeks and fry gently in butter for 5min then add to pumpkin.
- Add the egg, cheese and thyme to the pumpkin mix, season well and roll up in filo pastry.

Pizza Strudel

2 large onions, chopped
3 cloves garlic, crushed
500g tomatoes, chopped
300g Mozzarella cheese
50g black olives
Fresh basil and oregano
Salt & pepper
2 tbs olive oil

- Heat the olive oil in a frying pan and fry the onions and garlic for 5 mins.
- Add the tomatoes and fresh chopped herbs and stew for 10 mins. Cool.
- Take the stones from the olives and halve them, add to the tomato sauce along with the mozzarella cheese, cut into 2cm cubes.
- Roll up in filo pastry - you will have to use 2 sheets or the parcels will collapse.

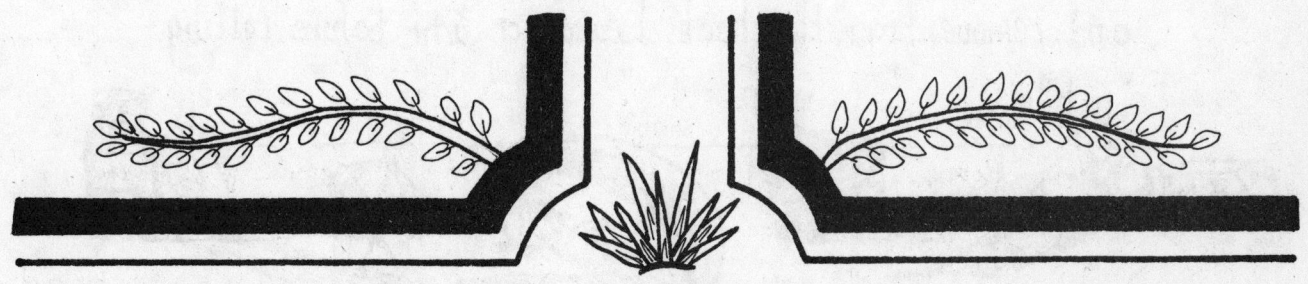

Madras Strudel

1 tbs Nuttelex
3 cloves garlic
1 cup onion
1 cup carrot
1 cup celery
1 cup green beans
1 banana

1 tsp. turmeric
1 tsp. cumin, ground
1 tsp. coriander, ground
1 tsp. paprika
½ tsp. cardamon, ground
1½ tbs. plain wholemeal flour
tamari to taste

- Dice the onion, carrot, celery and beans. Crush the garlic.
- Melt the Nuttelex in a large pan, add the garlic and cook slowly until translucent.
- Add the veggies and fry, stirring occasionally, for 5 mins.
- Stir in the spices, then the flour.
- Add enough stock or water to make a binding sauce - not too runny.
- Throw in the banana and cardamon, season with tamari, and remove from the heat. Leave for ½ hr before rolling in filo.

Spinach Triangles

1 bunch silverbeet, chopped
1 small onion, chopped
100g feta cheese, crumbled
1 egg
1 packet Filo pastry
100g unsalted butter, melted
Pinch nutmeg
Pinch pepper

- Whizz together the silverbeet, onion, feta, egg, pepper & nutmeg in a processor.
- Roll tablespoonfuls of the mixture into triangles.
- Bake at 200°C for 10-15 mins and serve hot with lemon and olives.

Spinach Pie

1 bunch silverbeet, chopped
1 onion chopped
500g cottage cheese
100g feta cheese, crumbled
2 eggs
Salt & pepper, pinch nutmeg
½ pkt filo pastry
50g unsalted butter, melted

- Mix together the spinach, onion, cottage cheese, feta, eggs and seasonings.
- Line a pie dish with sheets of buttered filo - use half the quantity - pour in the spinach mix, top with remaining buttered filo.
- Bake at 200°C for 20-30 mins until golden & flaky.

Tofu & Peppercorn Strudel

500g. tofu, cubed
75g. can green peppercorns
100g. mushrooms, sliced
2 cloves garlic, crushed
1 small onion, finely chopped
½ cup white wine
½ cup soya milk
¼ cup Nuttelex
¼ cup flour
1 packet filo
salt & pepper
100g unsalted butter or Nuttelex

- Melt the Nuttelex in a pan, add the onions & garlic and fry with a lid on for 5 mins.
- Add the mushrooms and fry for a further 5 mins.
- Add the flour, mix well, then pour in the wine and soya milk and simmer gently for five minutes.
- Finally add the tofu and peppercorns, season well and cool.
- Roll up in filo, as per instructions.
- Bake at 200°C. for 10-20 mins. until golden & crisp.

Green Peppercorn Strudel

500g. crumbled tempeh
50g. green peppercorns
100g. mushrooms, sliced
2 cloves garlic, crushed
1 small onion, finely chopped
½ cup white wine

½ cup soya milk
¼ cup Nuttelex
¼ cup flour
1 packet filo
100g. unsalted butter, melted
salt and pepper

- Melt the Nuttelex in a pan, add the onions & garlic and fry with a lid on for 5 mins.
- Add the mushrooms and fry for a further 5 mins.
- Add the flour, mix well, then pour in the wine and soya milk and simmer gently for 5 mins.
- Finally add the tofu and peppercorns, season well and cool.
- Roll up in filo, as per instructions.
- Bake at 200°c. for 10-20 mins. until golden and crisp.

Broccoli And Almond Filo

1 kg. steamed broccoli pieces.
250 g. lightly baked almond flakes
1 pkt filo pastry

Vegan White Sauce

250g. Nuttelex
1 cup flour
vegetable stock

2 cups soya milk
2 tsp. torula yeast
2 tsp. soy sauce
2 tsp. Dijon mustard

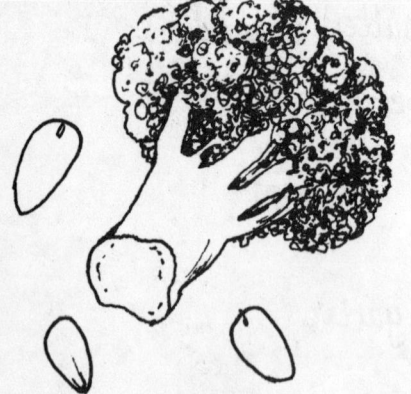

- Melt Nuttelex, blend in flour, cook.
- Take pan from the heat.
- Add the soya milk, yeast, soy sauce and mustard.
- Add vegetable stock as needed for required consistency.

- Add broccoli and almond flakes to white sauce and allow to cool.
- Roll mixture in filo and cook, as per instructions.

PROVENCAL STRUDEL

1 zucchini, diced
½ eggplant, diced
1 capsicum, diced
2 tomatoes, diced
1 pkt filo pastry
½ bunch fresh Sweet Basil, chopped
a few olives, chopped

1 onion, diced
1 clove garlic, finely chopped
250 g. mushrooms
50 g. tomato paste
pepper to season
½ bunch fresh Oregano, chopped

- Sprinkle chopped eggplant well with salt, leave for ½ hour, rinse thoroughly and pat dry.
- Sauté onions and eggplant until tender.
- Add remaining vegetables and seasonings and cook until still firm. Do not add water, drain off excess liquid if necessary.
- Carefully blend tomato paste with mixture, allow to cool.
- Roll the mixture in filo pastry, as per instructions for strudel.

The Art of GATEAUX Making

Our secrets for making gorgeous gateaux are few and simple, but make all the difference ~

* To keep the sponge moist and alcoholic so it doesn't absorb the moisture from the cream and leave it buttery.
* Don't use too much sugar in the cream or it will be too sickly and rich to eat.
* Keep the decoration simple but effective.

Here is the recipe for the basic sponge, which will make a 26cm diameter gateau ~ use a spring release tin if possible, oil it and line it with oiled greaseproof paper.

* The Sponge Cake ~ *

500g vegetable margarine
500g raw sugar
5 eggs

500g Self Raising wholemeal flour
A dash of milk

* Beat together the margarine and sugar, beat in the eggs one at a time.
* Fold in the flour gently with a dash of milk ~ don't overmix. Spoon into the prepared gateau tin.
* Bake at 180°C for 40-50 mins until spongy to the touch when pressed lightly in the middle.
* Turn onto a wire rack to cool.

Gateau Ideas

Black forest Gateau

- 700 mls cream
- 150g plain dark chocolate
- 1 large can sour or black cherries
- 4 tbs Kirsch liqueur
- 2 tbs Apricot jam

* Melt 100g chocolate with 2 tbs Kirsch and 50mls cream in a double boiler. Beat until smooth; leave to cool.

* Whip the remaining cream and set aside a small amount to pipe as decoration.

* Drain the juice from the cherries and keep ¾ cup juice; add the remaining kirsch to the juice.

* Split the gateau in half, and soak both halves with the juice. Spread the jam over the base half of the sponge. Arrange the cherries on top of the jam.

* Fold the chocolate into the cream and spread ⅓ over the cherries. Top with the other half of the sponge.

* Cover the sides and top with the remaining cream. Pipe rosettes of plain cream around the edge.

* Melt the remaining 50g chocolate and pipe fir tree shapes onto a sheet of greaseproof paper and chill well. Peel from paper and poke the trunk end into each rosette of cream.

** Use a chocolate sponge cake for this ~ replace 75g flour with 75g cocoa powder.

TIRA MI SU

LIQUEUR, CREAM-FILLED SPONGE FROM VENICE

INGREDIENTS
1 light egg sponge   or   a packet of Salvadore biscuit fingers.

FILLING
1 egg yolk   1 tsp. vanilla essence
3 tbs. icing sugar
250 gms. mascarpone or neufchatel cheese
(Try your Deli - or substitute 'Philly' cream cheese)

TO MOISTEN SPONGE
1 tbs. of Kahlua
1 cup of strong black coffee

COVER
Cocoa

° Mix ingredients of filling together smoothly.
  Cut sponge into thin layers.
° Put first layer on plate.
° Saturate sponge with coffee mixture.
° Cover with a layer of filling.
° Continue until each layer is on the plate.
° Cover the whole cake with the filling.
° Sprinkle the whole cake heavily with cocoa.

Cherry & Almond Strudel

2 cans stoned sour cherries
2 heaped tbs. cornflour
1 tbs. sugar

75 g. flaked almonds
2 tbs. Kirsch liqueur
½ pkt. Filo pastry
50 g. Nuttelex

- Drain the juice from the cherries, mix some with the cornflour, and heat the sugar, juice & cornflour until thickened. Cool.
- Mix the thickened juice, cherries and Kirsch and roll up 2 tbs. mixture in filo — see p.138 for method.
- Brush strudels with melted Nuttelex, sprinkle with flaked almonds and bake at 200°C. for 10-20 mins.

✳ Strawberry & Orange Gateau ✳

700 mls cream	2 oranges	4 tbs orange liqueur
3 punnets strawberries	3 tbs icing sugar	2 tbs strawberry jam

* Whip the cream and set some aside for decoration
* Select 12 nice even sized strawberries and save them; divide the remainder in half ~ puree one half and slice the rest.
* Grate the rind from 1 orange into the cream, juice both oranges and mix with 2 tbs liqueur. Soak the halved sponge in the juice, then spread the jam over the base. Arrange the sliced strawberries over the jam.
* Fold the remaining liqueur, icing sugar and strawberry puree into the cream. Spread 1/3 over the strawberries, top with the other half of sponge and cover with remaining cream.
* Pipe rosettes of plain cream around the edge and decorate with strawberries, orange slices and sprigs of dill.
** Use an orange flavoured sponge - add the grated rind of 2 oranges to the basic sponge.

✳ Coffee Gateau ✳ *Coffee Coffee*

700 mls cream	2 tsp instant coffee	2 tbs apricot jam
4 tbs coffee liqueur	1/2 cup black coffee	2 tbs icing sugar

* Split the sponge and soak in a mixture of 2 tbs liqueur and the black coffee less 2 tbs. Spread with apricot jam.
* Whip the cream and fold in the icing sugar, liqueur and instant coffee dissolved in 2 tbs black coffee. Use the coffee cream for filling, top and sides of gateau.
* Decorate with piped chocolate, chocolate covered peanuts, chopped hazelnuts and whipped cream rosettes.
** Use a coffee sponge - replace the milk with 1/2 cup strong coffee.

CHEESECAKE

500g cream cheese
1 egg plus 1 egg yolk
Finely grated rind of 1 lemon
50g sultanas
50g raw sugar
1 tsp vanilla essence
Filo pastry ~ p.138

- Allow the cream cheese to come to room temperature, then beat in all the other ingredients
- Roll in filo ~ either individual parcels or one large strudel. If making one large one, use about 8 sheets of filo, partially overlapping, and sprinkle a little cinnamon, sugar and ground almonds onto the butter between each layer of pastry.
- Bake at 180°C for 20-30 mins until golden.
- Serve cold and sliced thickly.

BARBADAD

4 ripe Cavendish bananas
150g dates
100g cream cheese
2 tbs rum
Filo pastry ~ p.138

- Cook the dates in 1 cup water until fairly mushy. Cool.
- Beat the dates and rum into the cream cheese, then slice the bananas and fold them into the mixture
- Roll into individual strudels and bake 15-20 mins until golden. Serve warm or cold.

Hazelnut Torte

250g margarine or butter
250g raw sugar
200g hazelnuts, toasted & finely ground
75g Self raising wholemeal flour
4 eggs, separated
½ tsp vanilla essence

300 mls cream
1 tsp instant coffee
1 tbs boiling water
1 tbs coffee liqueur, whiskey or Frangelico liqueur
1 tbs icing sugar

- Beat together the margarine and raw sugar, then beat in the egg yolks one at a time.
- Fold in the ground hazelnuts, flour and vanilla.
- Whip the egg whites until stiff and fluffy, then gently fold into the cake mixture.
- Oil and line with greaseproof paper a 20cm round, loose-sided cake tin. Pour in the cake mix and smooth the top.
- Bake at 180°C for 30-40 mins. Turn out cake and cool on a wire rack.
- Meanwhile, prepare the liqueur cream :- dissolve the instant coffee in the boiling water and cool.
- Whip the cream to soft peaks, then fold in the icing sugar, coffee and liqueur.
- Cut the cake into wedges, and serve with a big spoonful of liqueur cream on the side.

CHOCOLATE MOUSSES

600 mls cream
150g plain, dark chocolate
3 egg whites
3 tbs rum

- Melt the chocolate with 100 mls cream in a bowl over a pan of hot water. Beat until smooth then allow to cool. Beat in the rum.
- Whip the remaining cream until firm, then whip the egg whites until stiff.
- Fold together the chocolate mixture, cream and egg whites ~ you can reserve a little cream to pipe on top as decoration.
- Pile the mousse into delicate glasses ~ there should be enough for 6. Chill and decorate before serving.
- JAFFA MOUSSE ~ add the grated rind and juice of 2 oranges to the chocolate mixture and replace the rum with orange liqueur.
- CHOC~MINT MOUSSE ~ replace the rum with Creme de Menthe liqueur and garnish with after dinner mints.
- BLACK FOREST MOUSSE ~ replace the rum with Kirsch liqueur and fold in a drained tin of stoned sour or black cherries.

FRUITY MOUSSES
LEMON & HONEY

500mls cream   3 eggs, separated   3 tbs honey, or
3 lemons   1 tbs cornflour   more to taste

- Grate the rind of 1 lemon into a pan and add the juice of all three and heat gently.
- Mix the cornflour to a paste with 2tbs water, then whisk in the egg yolks. Stir this into the lemon juice and heat gently until thickened, stirring constantly.
- Remove from the heat, stir in the honey and leave to cool.
- Meanwhile, whip the cream until stiff, then whip the egg whites and when the lemon mixture is cool, fold everything together until smooth.
- Spoon or pipe into champagne glasses and serve chilled.

APRICOT

500mls cream, whipped   200g dried apricots   2tbs apricot brandy
3 egg whites, whipped   2tsp agar powder

- Soak the apricots in 500mls water overnight, then bring them to the boil and simmer 5mins. Cool, drain off 1 cup liquid, and reserve it; puree the fruit.
- Heat the cup of apricot liquid with the agar and simmer 2 mins, then mix into the apricot puree. Fold in the whipped cream, egg whites and apricot brandy.
- Spoon into glasses and chill before serving.

OTHER MOUSSES

MAPLE & WALNUT

500 mls cream, whipped   ½ cup maple syrup   ½ tsp vanilla essence
2 egg whites, whipped   1 cup finely chopped walnuts

- Fold all the ingredients together and pile into 6 glasses or dishes. Chill well before serving.

HAZELNUT & COFFEE

100g roasted hazelnuts   ¼ cup water   500 mls cream,
50g brown sugar   2 tsp agar powder   whipped
½ cup strong coffee   3 tbs coffee liqueur 2 egg whites, whipped

- Put the sugar, water and agar together in a pan and simmer for 2 mins. Remove from the heat and add the coffee, then leave to cool.
- Grind the hazelnuts in a proccessor until quite fine.
- When the agar mixture is cool enough to just begin to form a skin, fold together the whipped cream, egg whites, hazelnuts, agar mixture and coffee liqueur.
- Pile into tall glasses, chill and serve garnished with a few chopped hazels.

STRAWBERRY ROMANOV

3 punnets strawberries 3 tbs icing sugar
4 tbs Cherry Brandy 500 mls cream

- Wash and hull the strawberries. Slice 2 punnets into 6 tall glasses.
- Sprinkle the strawberries with 2 tbs icing sugar and 3 tbs Cherry Brandy.
- Puree the remaining strawberries, having first reserved 6 for decoration, then stir in the remaining 1 tbs icing sugar and 1 tbs (or more!) Cherry Brandy.
- Whip the cream then fold in the strawberry puree. Pipe the mixture into the glasses over the strawberries.
- Chill well and serve garnished with a sliced strawberry and a sprig of dill or mint.

BAKED BANANAS

For 4 lucky people you'll need 8 peeled Cavendish bananas ~ Lady Fingers don't cook so well.

Use either sauce, the method is the same

JAMAICAN

4 tbs dark rum
Rind & juice 1 orange
1 can coconut milk
50g butter
50g raw sugar

À L'ORANGE

4 tbs Cointreau liqueur
250 mls cream
Juice & rind 2 oranges
25g butter
50g raw sugar

- Melt the butter and brush the bottom and sides of a shallow baking dish liberally.
- Arrange the bananas in the dish.
- Mix together the remaining ingredients, including the melted butter and pour this over the bananas.
- Bake at 180°C for about half an hour, until the bananas are soft and golden.
- Serve hot with extra whipped cream for real decadence.

DATE SLICE

[it's cosmic!]

1 cup plain wholemeal flour
3/4 cup rolled oats
100g Nuttelex or other margarine
150g dates, chopped
50g chopped walnuts
1 cup water

5 Put the dates & water in a pan and simmer for 5 mins until mushy. Cool.
4 Rub the Nuttelex into the flour & oats.
3 Press the mixture into an oiled tray.
2 Spread the stewed dates over the base, then sprinkle the chopped dates over the top.
1 Bake the slice at 180°C for 20-30 mins.
BLAST OFF! Cool and cut into squares.

159

Pumpkin Pie

150g plain wholemeal flour
75g margarine or butter
2 tbs raw sugar
2-3 tbs cold water
500g cooked pumpkin
100g brown sugar
2 eggs
1 tsp ground cinnamon
½ tsp ground ginger
2 tbs brandy
300 mls cream

- First, prepare the pastry case :- rub the margarine into the flour, add the sugar and enough water to mix to a dough.
- Roll the pastry out on a floured board and line a 20cm diameter quiche or flan tin.
- To prepare the filling, whiz together the pumpkin, sugar, cream, eggs, spices & brandy until smooth.
- Pour the filling into the pastry case and bake at 180-200°C for about 30 mins until the filling has set.
- Serve warm or cold with extra cream.

CHOCOLATE COCONUT SLICE

Base:-
- 3/4 cup plain wholewheat flour
- 1 tsp baking powder
- 1 dessert spoon cocoa
- 75g butter, melted
- 1/4 cup raw sugar
- 1/3 cup coconut

Topping:-
- 3/4 cup icing sugar
- 1 dessert spoon cocoa
- 2 tbs condensed milk
- 3/4 cup coconut
- 30g melted butter
- 1/2 tsp vanilla essence

- To make the base, mix the dry ingredients together. Stir in the melted butter and press into an oiled baking tin ~ the shortbread should be about 1½ cm thick. Bake at 180°C for 20 mins.
- To make the topping, mix together the dry ingredients. Mix in the condensed milk, melted butter and vanilla.
- Spread over the base whilst still warm. Sprinkle with a little extra coconut.
- Refrigerate until set, then cut into squares and serve.

PINEAPPLE UPSIDE DOWN CAKE

250g butter or margarine
175g brown sugar
75g golden syrup
250g self raising wholemeal flour
3 eggs
1 pineapple
A handful of glacé cherries
A little extra butter & sugar to line the tin

- Thickly butter a 20cm, deep cake tin and sprinkle with a little sugar. Peel, core and slice the pineapple and arrange over the base of the tin. Fill any gaps with halved glacé cherries, then set aside.

- Next, prepare the sponge cake ~ cream together the butter, sugar and syrup. Beat in the eggs one at a time, then gently fold in the flour.

- Carefully spoon the cake mixture over the pineapple, then bake at 180°C for 40-50 mins until the cake is springy to the touch.

- Allow to cool in the tin for a few minutes, but turn out before the cake is completely cold or it will stick.

Ricotta-Cherry Cake

250g margarine
250g raw sugar
500g Ricotta cheese
4 eggs or 2 eggs & 2 yolks
200g S.R. wholemeal flour

50g ground almonds
1 tsp vanilla essence
½ tsp almond essence
Grated rind 1 lemon
1 can black or sour pitted cherries

- Beat together the margarine & sugar, beat in the ricotta cheese, then beat in the eggs, one at a time.
- Beat in the lemon rind, vanilla and almond essence then fold in the flour and ground almonds.
- Oil and line a 20cm round deep cake tin. Spoon in half the cake mixture and smooth over the base.
- Drain the juice from the cherries and scatter the cherries over the layer of cake mix. Spread the remaining cake mix over the cherries.
- Bake at 180°C for 40-50 mins until springy to the touch.
- Cool on a wire rack and dust with icing sugar to serve.

Pumpkin Cake

1/2 cup oil
1 cup honey
2 eggs
1 cup cooked, mashed pumpkin
2 cups plain wholemeal flour
1 tsp baking powder
1 tsp baking soda
1/4 tsp ground ginger
1 tsp nutmeg

2 tsp cinnamon
3/4 cup walnuts, chopped
3/4 cup raisins
Icing (optional)~
1 cup icing sugar
Juice & grated rind 1/2 lemon
2 tbs milk
1 tbs butter

* Beat together the honey and oil then beat in the eggs and pumpkin.
* Mix together all the dry ingredients and fold them into the pumpkin mixture, along with the raisins and walnuts.
* Pour the batter into an oiled and lined cake tin and bake at 180°C for about 1 hr until springy when touched in the centre.
* When the cake is cool, prepare the icing ~ heat the butter and milk together until melted. Mix the icing sugar and lemon rind and juice and add just enough of the melted milk & butter to form a spreadable icing.
* Swirl over the cake, leave to set then cut and serve.

Anna's Bancha Tea Cake

500g mixed dried fruit ~ dates, apricots & raisins
2 tbs cold pressed safflower oil
1 egg (optional)
2 tsp cinnamon
1 tsp ground coriander
1 cup Bancha tea
2 cups wholemeal flour
A pinch of salt.

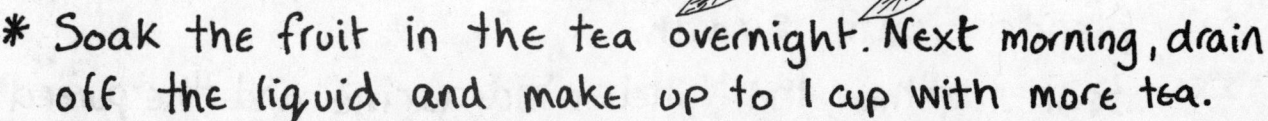

* Soak the fruit in the tea overnight. Next morning, drain off the liquid and make up to 1 cup with more tea.
* Roast the nuts in a medium oven until golden.
* Beat together the salt, spices, oil, liquid, then add the fruit and nuts. Add the egg, if using one.
* Fold in the flour, then pour into an oiled and lined loaf tin.
* Bake for 1 hour at 180°C.

Vegan date & walnut cake

250g Nuttelex
300g dates
1½ cups water
1 tsp cinnamon
½ cup walnuts
½ cup soya milk
350g S.R. wholemeal flour

✡ Put the dates in a pan with the water and simmer for 20 mins until mushy. Cool, then puree in a blender until smooth.

✡ Beat together the Nuttelex margarine and the pureed dates, then add the cinnamon and chopped walnuts.

✡ Fold in the flour and soya milk, then turn the mixture into a greased and lined loaf tin.

✡ Bake at 180°C for 40-50 mins, on a lower shelf, until just springy in the middle.

✡ Delicious hot or cold ~ it won't last long once tasted!

Carob Cake
(vegan)

3 cups wholemeal flour
2 tsp. baking powder
¾ cup cocoa or carob powder
¾ cup margarine

1 cup raw sugar
¼ cup hot water
2 cups soya milk
2 tsp. vanilla essence

- Cream margarine and sugar.
- Add vanilla and water and alternately flour and soya milk.
- Bake in a moderate oven for 45 minutes.

1 cup of margarine
1 cup of icing sugar

2 tsp. vanilla essence
½ cup of cocoa or carob powder

- Beat all ingredients together until light and creamy

CHOCOLATE RUM LOG

150g. plain cooking chocolate
1 tbs. vegetable oil or Nuttelex
3 tbs orange liqueur
3 tbs rum

150g. carob cake crumbs
50g. walnuts
50g. chocolate to coat the log
25g. Nuttelex to coat the log

- Melt the 150g. of chocolate in a bowl over hot water.
- Crumble the tofu and process with the oil, liqueur and rum. Work together until smoothly blended.
- Roll the mixture into a log in greaseproof paper and freeze.
- Take from freezer. Unwrap. Melt the remaining chocolate and Nuttelex and smooth over the log.
- Garnish with cherries or strawberries and mint leaves.

VICKI'S BICKIES
"they're Lifesavers!"

200g. Nuttelex
150g. raw sugar
300g. plain wholemeal flour
60g. sultanas
60g. cashew nuts
Finely grated rind of 1 orange

And a dash of soy milk.

- Cream together the Nuttelex and sugar.
- Add the sultanas, cashews and orange peel.
- Gently work in the flour, adding a bit of soy milk, to form a soft dough.
- Roll the dough out on a floured surface to 1cm. thickness.
- Cut out rounds and place them on an oiled baking tray.
- Bake at 200°C. for 10-15 mins until just getting a golden tinge.
- Cool on a wire rack and store in an airtight jar.

THE QUINTESSENTIAL CARROT CAKE

The Cake:—

1 cup grated carrot
1 cup plain wholemeal flour
1 tsp. baking powder
¾ tsp. bicarbonate of soda
¼ tsp. ground cloves
½ tsp. cinnamon
½ cup sugar
5 tbs. oil
½ cup chopped walnuts
400g. tin crushed pineapple, drained

The Icing:—

500g. Nuttelex
250g. icing sugar
½ tsp. vanilla essence

- Mix all the dry ingredients together, making sure there are no lumps of soda or baking powder.
- Add all the wet ingredients and the carrot, mix well.
- Pour into a greased and lined tin — we use loaf tins.
- Bake at 180°C. for 35 - 40 mins.

- Meanwhile, make the icing — beat the Nuttelex until soft, then beat in the icing sugar and vanilla.
- When the cake is cool, swirl the icing over the top of the cake and serve.

Flapjacks

125g margarine
50g honey
25g raw sugar
225g rolled oats
25g coconut
½ tsp vanilla essence
50g chopped dates

- Put the margarine, honey and sugar in a pan and melt over a low heat.
- Mix in the oats, dates, coconut and essence.
- Press into an oiled cake tin and bake at 180°C for about 20mins until golden brown.
- Cut into squares whilst still warm, but leave in tin until quite cold or the flapjacks will disintegrate when you try to get them out.

SWEET PASTRY

The same rules apply to making sweet pastry as to making savoury pastry....

250g plain wholewheat flour
125g vegetable oil margarine
50g raw sugar
cold water

- Mix the flour and sugar, rub in the margarine, and add the water to form a dough. The pastry is now ready to roll.

COCONUT SLICE

4 egg whites or whole eggs
100g raw sugar
100g desiccated coconut
2 tbs raspberry jam
½ quantity sweet pastry

- Whisk together the egg whites or eggs, and the sugar - they don't have to be too frothy. Mix in the coconut.
- Roll out the pastry to line a round or oblong baking tray.
- Spread the pastry with raspberry jam, then coconut mixture.
- Bake at 180°C for 20-25 mins.

Chocolate Square

250 g shredded wheatmeal cookies
50 g walnuts
50 g raisins
50 g plain cooking chocolate
75 g margarine
75 g golden syrup
75 g plain cooking chocolate to top

- Roughly crush the cookies — they don't have to be fine crumbs — and place in a bowl.
- Chop together the walnuts, raisins and 50g chocolate, and add to cookies.
- Melt the margarine and syrup together and pour into cookie mix. Stir well until the chocolate is melted and the crumbs are well coated.
- Press the mixture into an oiled tin to about 2cm thickness.
- Refrigerate until set, then melt the 75g chocolate in a bowl over hot water. Pour over the cookies and smooth the top.
- Refrigerate again, then cut in squares to serve.

MUFFINS

½ cup oil
½ cup honey
1 egg
1 cup milk
1 cup self raising flour, wholemeal

1 banana, mashed
50g chopped dates
A drop of vanilla essence
A pinch of cinnamon

- Whisk together the oil, honey and egg, then gradually whisk in the milk.
- Add the mashed banana, chopped dates, vanilla and cinnamon.
- Finally, gently stir in the flour until just combined in a batter.
- Oil some muffin tins and pour in the batter to just fill the tins.
- Bake at 200°C for 10-15 mins until well risen and just done.
- Serve straight from the oven with butter or cream and jam.

SWEET STRUDELS

Cherry & Ricotta

1 can sour or black pitted cherries
300g ricotta cheese
2 tbs kirsch liqueur
2 tbs raw sugar
50g toasted flaked almonds
Filo pastry - p138.

- Drain the cherries - if you like, you can make a sauce for the strudels with the juice. Add a little sugar and kirsch, and thicken with cornflour.
- Mix together the drained cherries, ricotta, kirsch, sugar and almonds.
- Roll the mixture into parcels and bake at 200°C for 10-15 mins until golden.
- Serve warm or cold with the cherry juice sauce and whipped cream.

APPLE

3 large green apples, peeled, cored and sliced
50g cake or breadcrumbs
½ tsp cinnamon
Rind of one lemon, finely grated
50g melted butter
25g raw sugar
50g sultanas
Filo pastry - p.138.

- Combine all the ingredients until the apple slices are well coated.
- Roll the mixture into small strudels or one big long one.
- Bake at 200°C for 10-15 mins ~ the larger one will take a little longer - turn the oven down to 180°C if it gets too brown. Serve hot or cold with lots of whipped cream.

TRIFLE

250g stale wholemeal cake
4 tbs sherry
1 can blueberries
1 can mandarins
250 mls milk
2 tbs custard powder
2 tbs sugar
250 mls whipping cream
grated chocolate, strawberries or chopped walnuts to decorate

- Crumble the cake roughly into a nice glass bowl.
- Drain off half the juice from the blueberries and mandarins, then pour the fruit and remaining juice over the cake. Spoon the sherry evenly over the fruit.
- Mix together the custard powder, sugar and 2 tbs of milk until smooth. Heat the remaining milk until boiling and pour over the custard mix, and return to the pan, stirring constantly. Heat gently until thick and bubbling.
- Pour the custard over the fruit and leave to cool.
- Whip the cream and pipe over the custard when cold.
- Decorate with grated chocolate, strawberries or walnuts.
- Chill for a couple of hours before eating, if you can wait that long!

Apple Crumble

750g green apples
½ tsp cinnamon
grated rind of ½ lemon
25g raw sugar

100g plain wholemeal flour
25g rolled oats
50g raw sugar
25g coconut
100g margarine or butter

- Peel, core and slice the apples, and put them in a pan with cinnamon, lemon and sugar, and 1cm depth water.
- Simmer gently for 10mins until just soft. Turn into an ovenproof dish.
- Put the flour, oats, sugar, coconut and margarine together in a mixing bowl and rub together lightly – the mixture should be a bit lumpy but not floury.
- Spread the crumble over the apples and bake at 180°C for 20-30mins until golden. Serve hot or cold with custard or cream.
- You can also use rhubarb, pears, peaches, apricots or plums instead of apples.

Bread Making

There's nothing more satisfying than mastering the art of bread making. Once you've produced your first crusty loaf and smelt it cooking you'll wonder why you didn't start years ago.

There are a few simple rules to ensure better bread baking ~ try to get fresh yeast rather than dried, develop a good kneading style so the dough has a good texture, and keep the dough moist but not wet.

Here is a basic bread recipe, with variations to follow.....

1 kg plain wholewheat flour
15g fresh yeast
1 tsp salt
50g gluten flour
Enough lukewarm water to form a firm, moist dough.

- Dissolve the yeast in 1 cup water.
- Mix together the flour, gluten flour and salt, make a well in the middle and pour in the yeasty water. Start mixing the dough with your hands, adding more water until you get a firm but elastic dough.
- Turn the dough onto a lightly floured board and knead for 3 mins until smooth. Set the dough back in the bowl, cover with a damp cloth or plastic bag, and leave in a warm place to rise for ½ hr or so ~ until it has risen and is nice and spongy.

- Turn the dough onto the board again and knead lightly. Divide the dough in two and knead each half into a short sausage.
- Oil two loaf tins and pop half the moulded dough into each tin. Put a damp cloth over the tops of the tins and leave in a warm place for about 20 mins, until the dough has almost doubled in size.
- Bake the loaves at 200°C for 30-40 mins, until the crust is brown and the loaf is cooked through. To test for doneness, turn the loaf out of the tins and tap the base ~ if it sounds hollow, it's done.
- Take the loaves out of their tins as soon as they come out of the oven and cool on a wire rack, to ensure a crispy crust.
- Hide until cool enough to slice and eat!

Malted Wheatberry

1 kg plain wholewheat flour
100g wholewheat grains
1 tsp sticky malt syrup
50g gluten flour
1 tsp salt
15g fresh yeast
Warm water

- Boil the wheat grains in just enough water to cover for 30 mins until the grains are soft. Remove from the heat, stir in the malt and leave to cool until lukewarm.
- Dissolve the yeast in one cup warm water.
- Mix together the flours and salt, stir in the wheat grains and malty cooking liquid, add the yeast and mix to a dough, adding a little more water if necessary.
- Proceed with the kneading and rising as for basic recipe. Bake for 40-50 mins at 200°C.

Rye & Caraway

500g plain wholewheat flour
500g rye flour
50g gluten flour
25g caraway seeds
1 tsp salt
½ tbs molasses
15g fresh yeast
Warm water to mix.

o Put the caraway seeds in a pan with 1 cup water and simmer for 5 mins. Remove from the heat, stir in the molasses and leave to cool until lukewarm.
o Dissolve the yeast in ½ cup water.
o Mix together the flours and salt, add the yeast and caraway mixture and form into a dough with a little more warm water if needed.
o Proceed as in basic bread recipe for kneading and rising. Bake at 200°C for 40-50 mins.

Grandma's Oat Loaf

100g rolled oats
1 cup milk
2 tbs molasses
1 kg plain wholewheat flour
1 tsp salt
15g fresh yeast
Warm water to mix.

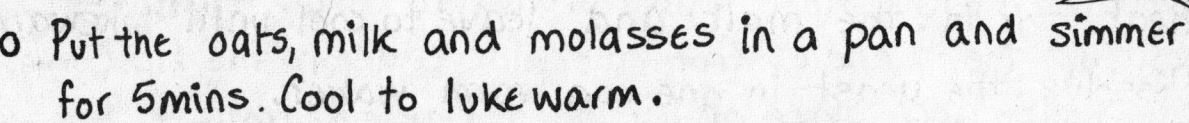

o Put the oats, milk and molasses in a pan and simmer for 5 mins. Cool to lukewarm.
o Dissolve the yeast in ½ cup warm water.
o Mix the flour and salt, add the oat mixture and yeast and mix to a dough with warm water. Proceed as for basic bread mix.
o Bake at 200°C for 30-40 mins.

Yeasted Pastry
Croissants

500g unbleached plain white flour
50g gluten flour
500g unsalted butter
20g fresh yeast
¼ tsp salt
Warm water to mix
1 egg, beaten, to glaze

- Dissolve the yeast in ½ cup warm water.
- Mix together the flours and salt, and rub in 25g butter. Add the yeast mixture and enough water to form a firm, elastic dough. Knead for 3 mins until smooth, then cover and leave to rise for 20 mins.
- Knead the dough lightly, then roll out to a thin rectangle. Dot with ⅓ butter, fold into 3, turn and roll out again. Repeat the rolling, buttering and folding until the butter is used, then roll and fold twice more.
- Cover and refrigerate for 20 mins.
- Roll out the dough to ½ cm thickness, cut into large squares, then in half diagonally to form triangles.
- Roll up the triangles from the wide edge to the tip. Curve the rolls and place on an oiled baking tray.
- Leave to rise in a warm place for 15-20 mins until growing in size. Brush with beaten egg.
- Bake at 200°C for 15~20 mins until golden and crispy outside, soft and succulent inside.
- Makes about 18 croissants.

Fruity Whirls

½ prepared croissant pastry
25g melted butter
25g raw sugar
75g mixed dried fruit
1 tsp mixed spice
½ tsp cinnamon
2 tbs apricot jam
2 tbs icing sugar
egg to glaze

- Roll out the prepared croissant pastry into a large rectangle ½ cm thick.
- Brush with melted butter, sprinkle the sugar, spices and dried fruit over the pastry, then roll up into a big sausage.
- Using a sharp knife, slice off 2cm rounds and place them, spiral side up, on an oiled baking tray. Brush with beaten egg and leave in a warm place for 15-20 mins.
- Bake at 200°C for 15-20 mins.
- Meanwhile, prepare the glazes ~ mix the icing sugar with 2 tbs water; mix the jam with 1 tbs water and heat until bubbling.
- As the buns come out of the oven, brush them first with apricot jam, then with the icing. Cool on a wire tray, or serve straight from the oven.

ODDS & ENDS

The Complement of Herbs

The herb chosen carefully for its fragrance and flavour will enhance any dish, from the simplest to the most exotic.

The emphasis of herbal usage has changed over the centuries, presumably since the comparative luxury of modern medicine. Before the days of penicillin and pain relievers, man, out of necessity, was very close to nature, and herbs were endowed with mystical as well as practical healing powers.

Nowadays, we can afford to enjoy these wonderful plants, not only for some of their undeniable medicinal qualities, but also for their aesthetics, their appeal to the senses, olfactory, visual and gustatory, and we can begin to appreciate the good taste of our forefathers.

Have you discovered what basil can do for tomatoes? There is something very special in the combination of thyme with mushrooms, aubergines or sweet potatoes; fennel goes well with cabbage, broad beans or pumpkin to name but a few.

Lemon balm makes you wonder what was extra special about that potato salad; tarragon is delicious in potato soup, and sorrel in lentil soup. Avocadoes are enhanced by lemon thyme, strawberries by fennel sauce, dill goes well with cucumbers, chervil in a soufflé.

Lemon balm with almonds makes a beautiful stuffing for apples, and carrot cake with lemon thyme will not be forgotten. The combinations are endless, the delicacies never cease to bring surprise and delight.

Just the aroma of a sprig of rosemary or basil at the side of a hot plate pleases the senses; borage flowers tossed through a green salad can not help but please the eye, stimulate the appetite and increase the enjoyment of a meal.

Jane Young
1983

Diana's Cumquat Jam

2 kg cumquats 1 kg raw brown sugar
water

- Rinse the cumquats and cut in half, removing the seeds – put the seeds in a little muslin bag.
- Put the fruit in a large pan, just cover with water and leave overnight.
- Bring to the boil & simmer until tender. Remove the muslin bag, then add the sugar and boil rapidly for about ½ hr until the jam will set.
- Fill sterile jars with the jam and cover.

Diana's Ginger Marmelade

8 oranges 250g ginger in syrup
1½ kg green apples, peeled & grated 50g ground ginger
2½ kg raw sugar water

- Wash oranges and shred finely – keep the seeds in a muslin bag. Cover with water and leave overnight.
- Bring to the boil and simmer until tender – remove seeds.
- Add the apples and simmer until water is well reduced.
- Add sugar and ginger and boil rapidly for ½ hr until the jam will set. Pour into pots and cover.

PEANUT BUTTER

The dressing:-
- 1 qty mayonnaise
- 2 tbs peanut butter
- 2 tbs lemon juice
- ¼ tsp chilli powder

The veggies:-
- 200g cooked wholewheat macaroni
- 3 med. zucchini, thinly sliced
- 2 apples, diced
- ½ med onion, finely chopped

- If you have a blender, whiz all the dressing ingredients together for a few seconds. If not, whisk them together with a fork.
- Prepare all the veggies, mix with the macaroni, and stir in the dressing. Chill and serve.

BANANA-PAPRIKA

The dressing:-
- 1 egg
- 1 tsp dijon mustard
- 1 clove garlic
- 1 tsp paprika
- salt & pepper
- 150 mls oil
- 2 tbs wine vinegar
- A pinch sugar

The veggies:-
- 250g bean shoots
- 2 med carrots
- 3 med bananas, sliced
- 100g roasted peanuts (not salted)

- In a blender, whiz the egg, mustard, garlic, paprika, sugar, salt & pepper
- Gradually dribble in the oil, then the vinegar.
- Cut the carrots in thin strips, mix all the veggies together, and toss in the dressing.

ORANGE & GINGER

- Juice & rind of 2 oranges
- 2 tbs tamari
- 1 cup water or veg. stock
- 1 clove garlic, crushed
- 1 small piece ginger, grated
- 1 tbs cornflour

= Mix the cornflour with 2 tbs water to a smooth paste

= Put the remaining ingredients in a pan, add the cornflour paste and heat to boiling, stirring often. Simmer for 5 mins.

= Serve over steamed vegetables as a side dish, or over stuffed vegetables for an unusual main course

= To add an Indonesian flavour, use coconut milk instead of the water.

HOT CHILLI HOT HOT

- 250g ripe tomatoes, chopped
- 1 tsp chilli powder or paste
- 2 cloves garlic, crushed
- 1 small piece ginger, grated
- Salt & pepper
- 1 tbs oil

= Put all the ingredients in a pan together and simmer for 20 mins.

= Whiz the sauce in a blender until smooth. Check the seasoning.

= Serve hot or cold ~ as a dip for spring rolls, sauce for tostadas, or condiment for curries.

WHITE SAUCE VARIATIONS

Basic =
500mls milk
25g butter
25g wholewheat flour

// Melt the butter in a pan, add the flour and cook for a minute.
// Add the milk, a bit at a time, beating well and bring to the boil between each addition.
// When all the milk is in, simmer for 5 mins stirring often. Season with salt & pepper to taste and use for one of the following sauces...

Cheese // Add 100g grated mature cheddar cheese, pinch of nutmeg and chilli and ½ tsp vegemite. Good for cauli, broccoli, pasta....

Capsicum // Fry 1 small, finely chopped onion and 1 thinly sliced red capsicum in 2 tbs butter. Add 50mls dry white wine, 1 tbs tamari and the white sauce. Good with cheese & walnut loaf.

// Green Peppercorn // Fry 1 small finely chopped onion in 2 tbs butter. Add 1 small tin green peppercorns, a dash of white wine, the sauce and 3 tbs cream. Good with loaves or burgers.

// Aurore // Add 2 tbs tomato paste, 2 tbs brandy and 50mls cream. Good for loaves or vegetables.

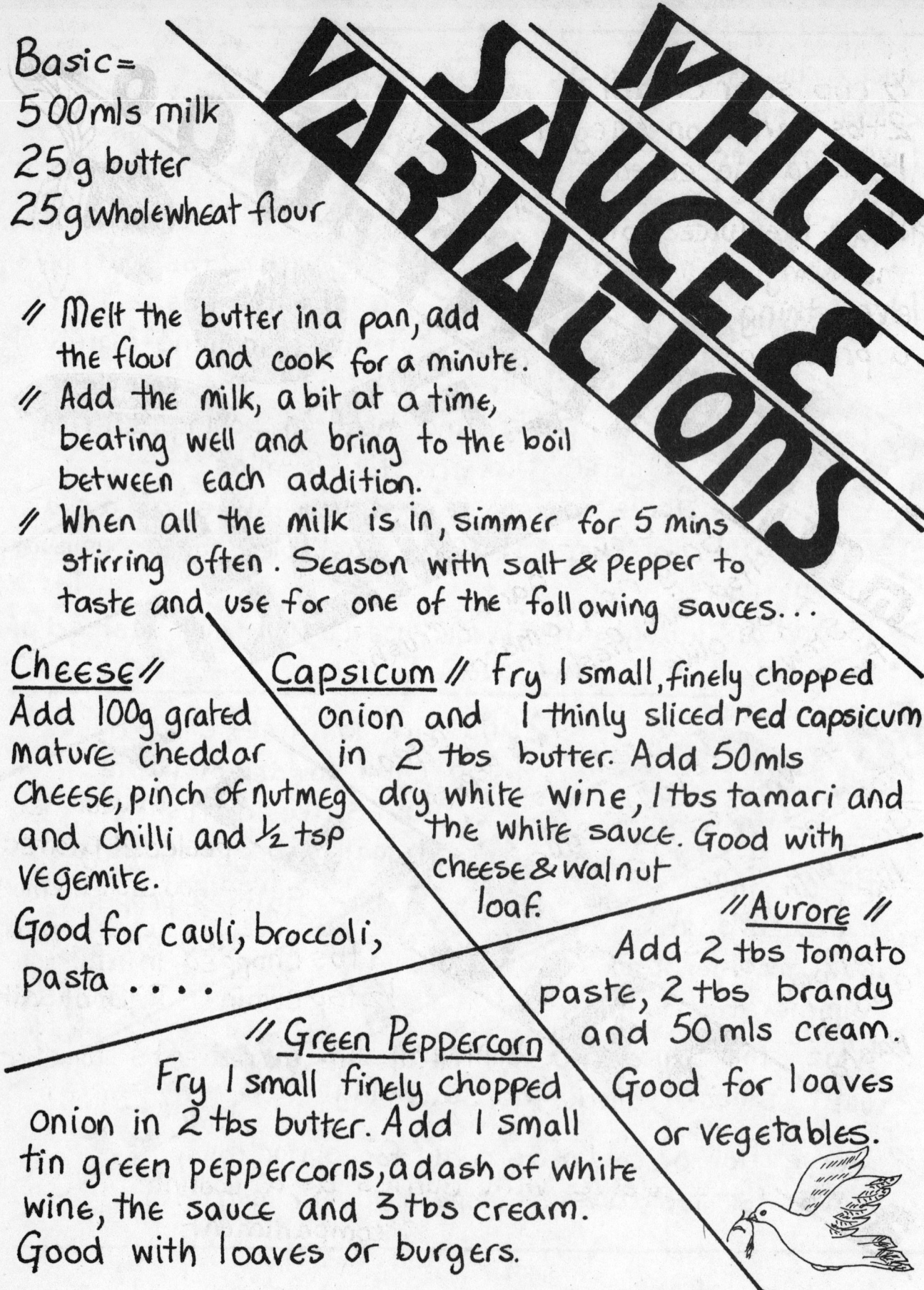

MANGO — "Good with avocados"

1 can mangoes
½ cup sour cream
2 tbs tarragon vinegar
1 tsp vanilla essence

= Drain the juice from the mangoes, whizz everything in a processor

FRESH TOMATO

2 cloves garlic, crushed
500g ripe tomatoes, chopped
1 tsp each fresh basil & oregano
2 tbs olive oil   Salt & Pepper

= Stew all the ingredients together for ½ hr. The sauce can be whizzed in a processor before use.
= Good with veggies like beans or cauliflower, also on pasta.

RAITA

1 cucumber, peeled & grated
1 cup natural yoghurt
1 clove garlic, crushed
1 tbs chopped mint
½ tsp cumin   Pinch of salt

= Mix all the ingredients together and leave to stand for at least 15 mins.
= Serve with curries as a cooling accompaniment.

WAYS WITH VEGGIES

ZUCCHINIS

are nice when cooked lightly in a sauce such as
- fresh tomato & garlic
- poach in a little white wine and cream.
- or saute in butter, garlic, salt & pepper.

CARROTS

Cut the carrots into interesting shapes ~

steam them until just tender and serve with any of the following ~
- a tablespoon of honey and a teaspoon of fresh grated ginger.
- 2 tablespoons of tamari and 2 tablespoons of sesame seeds.
- add a dash of sweet soy sauce - ketchap bentang.
- toss in 2 tbs butter 2 tbs fresh chopped herbs, salt & pepper.
- orange juice, salt & pepper.

CABBAGE

an underrated vegetable probably because it's usually over-cooked. Steam for 3 mins when finely shredded and serve with butter & black pepper, or ~
- stir fry in a little oil with coconut, paprika, turmeric and salt.
- stir fry with sliced onions, then add roasted peanuts & sultanas.
- stew gently with a little cider vinegar, chopped apple and currants, salt & pepper.

CAULIFLOWER, BROCCOLI & BEANS

Cauliflower and broccoli can be steamed as a whole head or split into florettes. Steam until the stems are just tender but still a little crunchy. Beans can be top & tailed and cooked whole or in pieces.

Any of the following sauces will go well with these veggies ~

~ mix together some sour cream, tomato paste, paprika, salt & pepper & a pinch of sugar and spoon over vegetables.

~ a creamy cheese sauce.

~ a white sauce with lots of chopped fresh herbs.

~ fry some fresh breadcrumbs in butter until crispy. Finely chop a couple of hard boiled eggs, add to the breadcrumbs, season, and sprinkle over veggies

~ top with an orange sauce.

~ top with a fresh tomato sauce.

TOMATOES

can be halved, placed on an oiled tray, sprinkled with Parmesan cheese and oregano, season, and grill or bake until the cheese is browned.

BRUSSELS SPROUTS

are traditionally served lightly steamed and tossed with cooked or canned chestnuts, butter, salt & pepper.

PARSNIPS

are delicious when roasted ~ cut into even size pieces, bring to the boil, drain and roast in oil for 30-40 mins until browned.

~ or try steaming parsnips lightly and tossing in butter with a little curry powder.

Ways with Potatoes

Sliced & Baked

Scrub potatoes and cut into ½ cm thick slices

Arrange in an oiled baking dish in an overlapping layer. Add seasonings, cover with foil and bake at 200°C for about 1 hr.

Suggested Seasonings
- sprinkle with sliced onions & cover with seasoned stock.
- brush with oil or ghee and sprinkle with garam masala.
- brush with oil or butter & sprinkle with herbs - rosemary or tarragon are very tasty.
- cover with a fresh tomato sauce.

Citrus Potatoes

500g potatoes, cubed
2 lemons, grated rind & juice
1 onion, finely chopped
50g butter   Salt & pepper

Fry the onion in butter until browning, add potato cubes and coat in butter. Add the lemon rind & juice, season well and spread on a baking tray. Bake for 40-60 mins at 180°C.

Potatoes Au Gratin

500g cooked potatoes
1 cup cream
100g grated cheddar cheese
Salt & pepper
Pinch of nutmeg & cayenne

Slice the potatoes into 1cm thick rounds. Arrange in a buttered baking dish in layers with half the cheese. Mix the cream & seasonings, pour over potatoes, top with remaining cheese and bake at 200°C for 20 mins

POMMES D'ARRAS

500g waxy potatoes, cubed
2 carrots, cubed
1 onion, chopped
2 cloves garlic, crushed
3 tbs olive oil
½ tsp thyme & rosemary
1 bay leaf
Salt & pepper

Heat the oil in a thick bottomed pan and fry the onions for 3 mins. Add the garlic & carrots, fry 2 mins, add the potatoes, herbs & seasonings. Top with a close fitting lid, reduce heat to very low and cook gently for 40-60 mins until potatoes are tender, stirring often to prevent sticking. Add a little water if the mixture gets too dry.

POMMES AUX POMMES?

500g potatoes
2 green apples, grated
50g currants
½ cup cream
25g butter
Pinch of cinnamon & nutmeg
Salt & pepper

Boil or steam the potatoes in their jackets until tender. Whilst still hot, mash with the butter & cream until smooth. Beat in the apple, currants, cinnamon & nutmeg, season and serve piping hot.

CARAWAY POTATOES

Potatoes
Salt, oil & caraway seeds

Cut potatoes in half, brush cut side with oil, place cut side down on an oiled baking tray. Sprinkle with caraway seeds & salt. Bake for 1-1½ hrs at 200°C until tender.

SAUTÉ POTATOES

500g waxy potatoes, cooked & chilled
3 tbs oil or butter
Salt & pepper
1 tsp paprika

Cut the potatoes into 1cm rounds. Heat the oil in a large frying pan, add potatoes & seasonings and toss over a high heat until browned.

Index

Agar agar	23	Beans, ways with	193	Cauliflower –
Almond –		Beans & Lentils	93	~ & curried soup	27
~ & green bean salad	69	Bickies, Vicki's	169	~ & broccoli soup	29
~ & veggy bake	104	Blackforest gateau	148	~ ways with	193
~ & broccoli filo	144	Brazilian stuffing	75	Cheese –
~ & cherry strudel	150	Bread making	179	~ dumpling casserole	87
Apple –		Broadbean pate	42	~ & walnut loaf	100
~ strudel	175	Broccoli –		~ sauce	190
~ crumble	177	~ & cauliflower soup	29	Cheesecake	152
Apricot mousse	155	~ & tomato salad	65	Cherry –
Arame salad	60	~ & walnut pie	78	~ & almond strudel	150
Aurore, sauce	190	~ & almond filo	144	~ & ricotta cake	163
Avocado –		~ ways with	193	~ & ricotta strudel	175
~ guacamole	38	Brussels sprouts, ~ ways with	193	Chick pea –
~ & lychee salad	52			~ greek	94
Banana –		Cabbage –		~ curry	113
~ barbadan strudel	152	~ ways with	192	Chilli –
~ baked à l'orange	158	Cannelloni –		~ beans with corn chips	109
~ jamaican	158	~ Caterina's	86	~ orange & ginger sauce	189
~ paprika	188	Capsicum sauce	190	Chocolate –
Bancha tea cake	165	Carob cake	167	~ mousse	154
Barbecue sauce	55	Carrots –		~ coconut slice	161
Bean goulash	110	~ & ginger salad	59	~ rum log	168
Bean shoots –		~ cake	170	~ square	173
~ salad	64	~ ways with	192	Coconut –
~ & tempeh salad	69			~ chocolate slice	161
				~ slice	172

Coffee –	Fennel & orange	Green bean –
~ gateau 151	salad 67	~ salad 66
~ & hazelnut mousse 156	Fettucini & tomato	~ & almond salad 69
Coleslaw 68	sauce 56	Green peppercorn
Coriander balls,	Filo –	~ strudel 143
tofu 39	~ pastry 23, 138	~ sauce 190
	~ broccoli & almond 144	Guacamole 38
Corn chowder 34	Flapjacks 171	Hazelnut –
Cous cous –	Fried rice & tofu	~ torte 153
~ general 23	teriyaki 129	~ & coffee mousse 156
~ casablanca 121	Fritters, vegetable 92	Hejiki 23
Cream cheese	Fruity whirls 183	Herbs, general 185-186
& pumpkin 139		Honey & lemon
Croissants 182	Gado gado 49	mousse 155
Cucumber salad 63	Gateaux –	Hummus 41
Cumquat jam 187	~ making 147	Hungarian –
Curry casserole,	~ ideas 148	~ mushroom soup 32
Cath's 117	~ blackforest 148	~ paprika soup 35
	~ strawberry & orange 151	Indian –
Date –	~ coffee 151	~ salad 59
~ slice 159	Ginger –	~ stuffing 75
~ & walnut cake 166	~ & carrot salad 59	Indonesian stuffing 73
Dhal 115	~ marmalade 187	Iranian pilau 119
Diets 19-20	~ & orange chilli	Irish stew
Dill & zucchini	sauce 189	& potato dumplings 81
soup 30	Gluten 23	Italian stuffing 74
	Gnocchi 80	
Eggplant –	Greek –	Kombu 23
~ dumplings 88	~ melon salad 60	Lasagne 84
~ & potato curry 116	~ salad 66	Lebanese –
Falafel 107	~ chick peas 94	~ stuffing 72

~ pilau   120
Leek ~
  ~ & potato soup   31
  ~ & sweet potato
         loaf   105
Lemon & honey
       mousse   155
Lemongrass & tofu
       curry   112
Lentil ~
  ~ pie, sherwood   95
  ~ pie, Bronwyn's   96
  ~ burgers   97
  ~ & zucchini khoreshe   98
  ~ loaf   99
Lentils & beans   93
Lychee & avocado
       salad   52
Madras strudel   140
Mango & tomato
       raita   191
Maple & walnut
       mousse   156
Mexican stuffing   75
Minestrone   28
Mirrin   23
Miso ~
  ~ general   22
  ~ & green vegetable
         soup   25
Moussaka   89
Muffins   174

Mushroom ~
  ~ dried   22
  ~ hungarian soup   32
  ~ triple soup   33
  ~ pate   40
  ~ brochette   43
  ~ stuffed   48
  ~ sauce   57
  ~ salad   62
  ~ & tofu on spinach
         pasta   85
  ~ loaf   102
  ~ punjabi   114
Nicoise salad   65
Nori   22
Nut ~
  ~ terrine   101
  ~ loaf, Nick's   103
Nuttelex   23
Oat loaf, grandma's   181
Orange ~
  ~ & fennel salad   67
  ~ & strawberry
         gateau   151
  ~ & ginger chilli
         sauce   189
Paprika ~
  ~ hungarian soup   35
  ~ banana   188
Parsnips, ways with   193
Pasta salad   67
Pastry ~
  ~ sweet   172
  ~ yeasted   182

Pea soup, split   26
Peanut butter   188
Peanut sauce with
       tofu satays   125
Peppercorn & tofu
       strudel   142
Pilau ~
  ~ iranian   119
  ~ lebanese   120
Pineapple upside
       down cake   162
Pizza ~
  ~ pita   82
  ~ zucchini based   90
  ~ strudel   139
Plum sauce   23
Potato ~
  ~ & leek soup   31
  ~ salad   61, 68
  ~ dumplings &
         irish stew   81
  ~ & eggplant curry   116
  ~ sliced & baked   194
  ~ citrus   194
  ~ au gratin   194
  ~ pommes d'arras   195
  ~ caraway   195
  ~ pommes aux
         pommes   195
  ~ sauté   195
Provencal strudel   145
Pumpkin ~
  ~ souffle   91
  ~ honeyed   111
  ~ & cream cheese   139
  ~ pie   160

~ cake 164
Quiche provencal 77
Raita 191
Rice -
~ asian 106
~ fried, with tofu teriyaki 129
Ricotta -
~ & spinach pie 79
~ & cherry cake 163
~ & cherry strudel 175
Russian tartlets 45
Rye & caraway bread 181
Savoury pies & pastries 76
Soya -
~ mayonnaise 53
~ sour cream 53
Soyaroni marinara 83
Spinach -
~ & ricotta pie 79
~ pasta with tofu & mushroom 85
~ & tofu pie 123
~ loaf & tofu 124
~ pie 141
~ triangles 141
Spring rolls 46
Strawberry -
~ & orange gateau 151
~ Romanof 157
Stuffings 71-72

Swedish casserole 108
Sweet potato & leek loaf 105
Tabouleh 64
Tahini -
~ general 22
~ sauce 54
Tamari 21
Tempeh -
~ general 21, 133-34
~ & beanshoot salad 69
~ sweet & sour 135
~ kebabs 136
~ burgundy 137
Thousand island dressing 52
Tira mi su 149
Tofu -
~ general 21, 122
~ chinese soup 37
~ coriander balls 39
~ & mushroom on spinach pasta 85
~ & lemongrass curry 112
~ & veggie curry 118
~ & spinach pie 123
~ & spinach loaf 124
~ satays with peanut sauce 125
~ chinese style 126
~ 'a la king 127
~ battered, in sweet & sour sauce 128
~ teriyaki & fried rice 129
~ chow mein 130

~ nuggets in chick pea batter 131
~ loaf, curried 132
Tomato ~
~ & zucchini soup 36
~ & fettucini sauce 56
~ & broccoli salad 65
~ & mango raita 191
~ ways with 193
Torula yeast 23
Tostadas 44
Trifle 176
Vegetable fritters 92
Vinaigrette 51
Vine leaves, stuffed 47
Waldorf salad 63
Walnut ~
~ & broccoli pie 78
~ & cheese loaf 100
~ & maple mousse 156
~ & date cake 166
Wheat salad 62
Wheatberry bread 180
White sauce & variations 144, 190
Zucchini ~
~ & dill soup 30
~ & tomato soup 36
~ pizza 90
~ & lentil khoreshe 98
~ ways with 192